Also by Joseph F. Girzone

Joseph F. Girzone

THE TRUE STORY OF
ONE BOY'S RELATIONSHIP
WITH GOD

Doubleday
New York   London   Toronto   Sydney   Auckland

Published by Doubleday
a division of Bantam Doubleday Dell Publishing Group, Inc.
1540 Broadway, New York, New York 10036

Doubleday and the portrayal of an anchor with a dolphin are
trademarks of Doubleday, a division of Bantam Doubleday Dell
Publishing Group, Inc.

Book design by Joseph M. Duraes

Library of Congress Cataloging-in-Publication Data

ISBN 0-385-48282-0
April 1997
First Edition
1   3   5   7   9   10   8   6   4   2

This story about a young boy

is dedicated to his family:

Richard, his father;

Elizabeth, his mother;

Rick, Mike, John and Pete, his brothers.

Their pain is eased only by the

memories of the music that flowed from

his soul.

Introduction

THE TINY SPARK OF LIFE in its mother's womb has, within its almost microscopic existence, the coded material that will evolve into a masterpiece of incredible proportions. The story that follows is about a young boy, a boy I knew from childhood, whose life would unfold into a magnificent adventure, a boy who was born with a smile on his face and music in his heart, a boy who was to reflect all that the young people of our times experience: the wonder of existence, the adventure of discovery, the joy of new love, the pain of betrayed trusts and broken commitments, the dreams of youth that we all cling to until they slip through our fingers, the endless search for a meaning to life and its endless riddles, and the joy of finding a wonderful God who can bring all these complex facets of life into focus, giving significance to all the apparently unrelated loose ends of our life. This story is about a rare and beautiful love affair between a young boy and God. I pray it gives hope to young people and comfort to mothers and fathers who watch fearfully as their children enter the unknown world of life's adventure.

Joey

One

D O YOU KNOW THE MUFFIN MAN, the Muffin Man,
the Muffin Man? / 'Do you know the Muffin Man
who lives on Drury Lane?' / 'Yes, I know the Muffin
Man, the Muffin Man, the Muffin Man. / 'Yes, I know
the Muffin Man who lives on Drury Lane.' " So sang
Joey Della Ratta as he half-walked, half-skipped down
Wendell Avenue on his way home from school. He
was five then. His singing was the key to understanding the rest of his life.

At that time I was still Joey's best friend. He
had been named after me, Joseph Francis. I had bap-
tized him, babysat for him, said his prayers with him,

taught him many things as a little child. Once he reached six, though, he started making friends at school and in the neighborhood, bringing all kinds of kids home with him. Skin color, nationality, family background, made no difference. He loved everyone and everyone loved him, boys and girls, teachers and principals, music teachers and baseball and hockey coaches. His deep brown eyes sparkled with an impish playfulness that only thinly veiled the vast world of adventure lying beneath the surface of a mind that was as complex as it was mischievous—a world no one could ever penetrate. It was almost as if he lived two lives, the one on the surface, a happy life, which everyone saw; and the other behind the veil, which no one was ever allowed to see, except in rare, fleeting moments. That life was a life of extraordinary depth, and mostly painful, where there developed a spirituality at once unexpected and quite extraordinary in one so young.

Let me tell you the story of his life. I was a priest at Our Lady of Mount Carmel church in Schenectady, New York, when a young boy named Johnny rode down the street to the rectory and asked if I would like a ride on his tricycle. I was thrilled that he asked. We became longtime friends. He is now in law school and on vacations spends his time painting my house. This little tyke often visited his grandparents who lived two doors from the rectory, in the Mount Pleasant section of the city. Their names were Pete and Angie Della Ratta. Pete's homemade wine was the best in the area, except maybe for that of another friend, Dominick Leone. As Pete got older, turning the press became too much of an effort. He asked me to help him. I was honored. I wanted to learn how to make wine anyway and now was my chance. We became good friends.

Occasionally Pete and Angie's son and daughter-in-law would visit on Sunday. Dinner after Mass was always a feast in an Italian home, and being invited to the Della Rattas practically every Sunday was a treat. In time they became like a second family to me. Pete and Angie's son, Richard, and his wife, Elizabeth, were in their thirties. Richard was a lawyer and president of the city school board at the time. Liz was a nurse, but with three boys already and another child on the way, she thought it better to take a leave of absence and become a full-time mother. Not that she was old-fashioned: she was already liberated and looked upon being a mother as her chosen career.

A few months later Joey was born, a beautiful, happy baby with big brown eyes. On the day of his baptism he looked like an angel. I was proud his parents had named him after me and given me the privilege of channeling to him a share in God's life.

I don't remember much of Joey's very early years, except his happy, playful spirit and, at times, a thoughtfulness that struck me as unusual. My real recollections of him begin when he was a little older.

One evening when Joey was three and a half, I stopped at the house for dinner. As soon as I came in, he ran over to hug me and asked if he could camp at my house. "Why would you want to do that?" I replied.

"Because my brothers went camping and I was told I am too small to go," was his answer.

"I guess it's all right. Sure, Joe, you can go camping at my house anytime."

"Thank you, Fahd." And that was that.

We had a delightful supper that night and chatted about school board problems. Richard was always trying to figure out ways of bettering the lot of the teachers, whose salaries at the time did not compare favorably to those of teachers in other areas.

Later, when I was leaving, Richard and Liz walked me to the front door. I was surprised to see Joey sitting on the stairs in the foyer, dressed in his pajamas, sucking his thumb, his packed airline bag lying next to him. He was sound asleep.

As I opened the door, he woke up and said, "Are we all ready, Fahd?"

"For what, Joe?"

"Remember, I'm going camping at your house tonight."

I looked questioningly at his father and mother. Richard grinned and said, "Well, you promised him."

"Okay, Joe, let's go."

I picked him up and carried him out to the car while he hung on to his airline bag. He was so happy.

When we arrived at the rectory, which was only a few miles away (in Scotia, where I had been transferred), I carried him into the house and went to the kitchen for a little "party." For Joey, a party meant an ice cream soda, which I later realized he shouldn't have had before going to bed.

He, however, was thrilled. "Fahd, this is the best party!"

"It's fun, isn't it, Joe?"

He looked at me and beamed.

When we finished, I took him up to bed. There were no provisions in the rectory for visitors, so I plopped him down on my bed. Since I don't usually move around much in my sleep, I figured it would be big enough. However, in the middle of the night, I woke up to find myself soaking wet. I felt the bed; it was saturated.

I nudged Joey. Looking at me with his big brown eyes, he asked, "What happened, Fahd? Did we have an accident?"

"Yeah, I guess we did, Joe. You had better get up and change while I wash the bed and change the sheets." The rest of the night was restful.

The next morning after we got up and dressed, I brought him to the church with me. It was a weekday, so it wouldn't be too busy. Usually, only about forty or fifty people showed up at morning Mass.

When I finished vesting, I told Joey just where to sit on the side of the sanctuary. He went out and sat there, sucking his thumb all during Mass, eyeing everything in sight. When Mass was over, he had a thousand questions.

Walking me across the sanctuary to a large, almost life-size crucifix, he asked, "Fahd, what is that?"

"That's a crucifix, Joe."

"Who's that on the cross?"

"Jesus."

"What's that in his hands and feet?"

"Nails."

"What's that on his head?"

"A crown of thorns."

"What's that in his side?"

"That's where a soldier thrust a spear through his heart."

"Why did they do that to him? What did he do wrong?"

"Nothing, Joe. He was just so good, some powerful people couldn't stand him; so they decided to get rid of him."

Joey was silent. I looked down at him and tears were streaming down his cheeks. I didn't realize it then, but in that brief encounter that little boy fell in love with Jesus. Every time he came over to camp at my place, he would stare in silence at that image of Jesus.

One day after Mass he asked me, "Fahd, when the people come up the aisle and hold out their hand, what's that cookie you give them?"

"Joe," I explained with a smile, "that's not a cookie; it's Jesus."

"Fahd, can I have Jesus? I love him so much."

"You have to be seven to make your first Communion."

"Oh!" he said with sadness in his eyes.

I felt bad. "Joe, I'll tell you what I'll do. I'll give you a make-believe Jesus before Mass and you can close your eyes and talk to Jesus. He'll come close to you and bless you."

That satisfied him for a while, and every time he came over camping, he would look forward to having Jesus in the form of an unconsecrated wafer. It was important to him. Jesus had really become his friend.

About a year and a half later, when he was visiting and we were at the church for Mass, I took an unconsecrated wafer from the container and offered it to him as I had many times before. His response caught me off guard. "Fahd, I don't want the make-believe Jesus anymore. Why can't I have the real Jesus? He's my best friend and I love him so much."

"Joe, you have to be seven," I reminded him.

"Fahd, what's so magic about seven. I love Jesus and I'm only five."

"Well, I guess nothing, Joe." His insight into a Church rule that didn't make much sense to him threw me, and made me realize that in his case it did *not* make much sense. "Let me talk to your mother and father and see what they say."

I did talk to Elizabeth and Richard. They were surprised. Joey kept so much to himself that they hadn't realized how he felt. However, when I explained what I had been doing for the past year and a half, they gave their approval, though I think they still found it hard to believe that a boy so young could feel so strongly about God.

So, at five years of age, against a centuries-old

custom of the Church, Joey received his first Holy Communion, together with Joe Bashant, my nephew, another precocious little boy with an inquisitive mind and a sensitive soul. It was the occasion of a momentous encounter with Jesus that profoundly touched those two young boys. It was also an unforgettable day for their families. From then on Joey rarely missed Communion and never made a fuss over going to church on Sunday mornings.

On the outside, Joey's life was normal. But his feelings, even about Jesus, he kept to himself. He loved to play, and at about that time he started making friends at school and in the neighborhood, Nick Petruccione, for one; Sarah Zuckerman, Kent Johnson and George Bull were others. They were inseparable. Once Joey found friends he could play with every day, he lost interest in camping at the rectory. I felt a little bad, but realized it was healthy for him to have playmates as daily companions. Once in a while he would still come to the rectory to stay overnight, mostly when his parents needed a babysitter. When he did so, it was a joy to give him Holy Communion. As young as he was, it meant so much to him. After receiving the Eucharist, he would just sit there quietly thinking about Jesus' presence within him and talking to him about his own little world of fun and troubles.

Being close to the Della Ratta family, I was

able to have an influence on the children's religious life. Michael and I built a hut in the backyard from old lumber in the cellar. After twenty-six years, it is still standing. Michael also served Mass, while his brother Rick played the organ occasionally at Our Lady of Mount Carmel in Amsterdam when I was pastor there. He also played the organ at St. Joseph's in Scotia after I had left.

Molding the children to have a deep sense of Jesus was important. And it was particularly important that they develop a warm relationship with Jesus as a friend, something they could treasure all their lives.

My parents had taught me to be close to Jesus, but during my childhood I was also given a heavy dose of the judgmental God. So, even though I had a warm relationship with Jesus, this rigid, legalistic approach to religion acted like a straitjacket and paralyzed my ability to expand my vision. My concept of holiness was to dream of being like someone else—St. Francis; or Father Damien, the priest who worked among the lepers; or later on, St. Athanasius, the bishop who alone defended the true nature of Christ at a time when almost the whole Christian world, including the emperor and many bishops, had succumbed to the Arian heresy. The road to holiness was the road to self-perfection and personal heroism. The simplest way to accomplish this was to imitate one of the saints in the way he had lived out his love of God. It never occurred to me that the road to true holiness lies not in imitating someone else, however inspiring that person's life may be, but in allowing God into our lives and together developing the vast possibilities that lie within ourselves.

Each of us is a unique creation designed to fill a necessary role in the unfolding of God's plan for humanity. We are not created in a vacuum to work out our own personal holiness totally unrelated to the world around us. "Come, blessed of my Father into the kingdom prepared for you. When I was hungry you gave me food, when I was thirsty you gave me drink, when I was naked you clothed me . . ." God created the world as a highly intricate network of relationships, with everyone and everything interdependent in the unfolding of His creation. It is not just our own perfection God has blueprinted, but the overall perfection of the living universe itself. In watching an ant go about its daily chores in the accomplishment of its individually appointed task, we realize that what the ant does is important not so much in itself but for what it contributes to the overall purpose of the colony: the creation of an environment in which all the members can live and function efficiently. I learned only fairly late in the game that my own growth in holiness was linked to understanding—or, if I did not fully understand, at least to cooperating in—the work God had created me to accomplish, whatever it might be. I realized I could find the key not only to happiness and an uncontrived holiness but to undreamed-of adventure as well. I wanted to share this with Joey at an early age so that he would not have to labor for countless years wondering what this life is all about.

Joey's falling in love with Jesus was, I think, a rare grace from God. It set the framework for his whole spirituality, a spirituality based not on the ever-conscious observance of religious law, with all its judgmental implications, but on living out his relationship with Jesus, who was his very real best friend. This friendship was like a shining star that showed him the way. It even affected how Joey made his decisions and generated a simple means for solving problems.

One day Joey had taken his brother Rick's treasured baseball, which was covered with signatures of famous players. After playing a game with it, he noticed that all the autographs had rubbed off. He felt horrible. The next day was Sunday. As he sat in church thinking about what he had done, he felt unworthy to take Communion. In the old days many of us would have asked ourselves, "Did I intend to steal the ball or just borrow it? If I intended just to borrow it, that would probably not be a sin. If I intended to take it for good, that would be stealing and that *would* be a sin. Would it be a big sin, really offensive to God, or just a little sin? Now, if the ball was worth a lot of money, then it could be a big sin and I would have to go to confession. With all those names on it, it really was valuable." And so on.

Joey had no such problem. Jesus for him was as real as if he were sitting next to him. So he talked to him. "Jesus, I did something terrible yesterday. I took my brother's baseball and played a game with it. It had all the players' autographs on it, and they were all rubbed off when we finished. I feel bad, Jesus, and I know I should be good when I go to Communion, but I can't go through the whole week without receiving you in my soul. If I can go to Communion, when I go home I promise I'll tell my brother what I did and apologize to him. I know he's going to be really mad at me, but that's okay, Jesus. I want so much to receive you in Communion." Then he went to Communion. It was so simple.

One day when he came home after school, he was acting particularly happy. His mother asked him why. "Because I did something today in school that I knew Jesus would have wanted me to do. There's a girl in class whom everyone ignores. She's rather slow. She always looks so sad, so, during play period, I asked her if she would dance with me. She was thrilled. The other kids laughed at me, but I didn't mind. I knew I made Jesus happy."

Reading these little stories, one might get the impression Joey was a quiet, introverted boy, but he was just the opposite. He was fun-loving and full of mischief. At the time, I was chairman of the Human Rights Commission for the area, and after finishing work at the office, I would stop over at the Della Rattas'. Frequently Joey would be walking home from school just then. When he noticed me getting out of the car in front of his house, he would run down the street as fast as he could. I'd be standing there waiting for him. When he was a few yards away, he would leap into the air with arms and legs outstretched for me to catch him. He wasn't more than six. That was the way Joey threw himself into life, with total abandon and absolute trust.

After school the kitchen often smelled of pies or cookies baking in the oven. Joey and his brothers loved that. Joey would be all upset if the house was empty when he got home from school. It was a big letdown and he would tell his parents how sad he felt when no one was there. Seeing the effect it had on Joey made me think about the many kids who never experience a mother or father waiting for them at home, or who never smell pies or cookies baking in the oven. These things can contribute a lot to a child's sense of security and well-being, and create warm, nostalgic memories for the future. They make a child feel loved, and as if he or she is important to the parents.

It was at about this time that Joey began to take music lessons. Elizabeth and Richard were both musicians. Richard played the French horn, and Liz played the piano, as well as the organ at church. Joey's older brother Rick was at the time studying piano; he later graduated from the New England Conservatory and launched a successful musical career. Joey himself started out with piano lessons.

The first year and a half brought what every family endures when a member starts lessons. As good as Joey was, he was still a beginner and the endless exercises were painful for everybody. Once Joey got the feel of the instrument, however, he was like a fish in water. His fingers began to move along the keys like magic. Knowing how moody he could be, I told him one day to go to the piano whenever he was sad or happy and just make up his own music. "It would be a good outlet for your feelings and a way of praying to God." He gradually learned to do that, and whenever he was hurting, he would go to the piano and play his heart out. I always knew by the way he played when something was troubling him, and would ask him as he was playing, "Joe, what is it that's troubling you?" But he would just say, "Nothing, Fahd." I always felt bad that he could never share his pain, though as he got older, he would share a few things— but never in any depth.

Two

W<small>HEN</small> J<small>OE</small> (<small>AS</small> I <small>THEN STARTED TO CALL HIM</small>) was
five years old, his brother Peter was born. He
was a funny boy with his mind already made up when
he arrived. He knew just what he wanted and just what
he did not want, especially when it came to food. If he
did not like something, it could sit untouched on his
highchair tray for hours. He baffled Joe no end. At
times I'd catch Joe looking askance at Pete out of the
corner of his eye, as if to say, "What's up with this
kid?" From the first day on they were competitors. Joe
was at a disadvantage, however, since he was easygoing
and lovable. Pete was lovable, too, but he could be

pushy and demanding. Joe would just give up and walk away. That was the way he reacted to all unpleasant situations. Whenever there was turmoil in the house or a noisy situation, Joe would quietly slip out the front door and disappear until the storm passed.

At about this time I was transferred to Our Lady of Mount Carmel parish in Amsterdam, New York. It was my first pastorate. The parishioners were for the most part rugged, down-to-earth folk with just ordinary jobs, many of them retired from the city's big carpet mills. I learned to love these people. They were the salt of the earth. They are the characters in my *Joshua*. We had the most wonderful times in that parish. The first thing I did was to turn it over to the people and let them run it. I was content being their spiritual director. Treating them this way, I had more authority than any pastor could hope for. They made sure the decisions they made were not in the slightest way offensive to me. At one time, when the state took over the local synagogue to build a highway, the parish council voted unanimously to start a fund-raising drive to rebuild the synagogue. Since there were only a few Jewish families in the area, the money from the state was not enough for them to rebuild. The relationship between the parish and the synagogue was so intimate that we were the closest thing to a merger between a Jewish and a Catholic community in two thousand years. At Christmas each year Emmanuel Rosen and his wife (from the synagogue) gave my housekeeper huge bagsful of toys for our Santa Claus (our mailman), who used to ride through our parish in an antique horse-drawn sleigh on Christmas Eve giving out presents to all the children waiting along the streets for him. The grandparents got the biggest thrill just standing with the kids and watching the wonder on their faces. Once, Santa got out of the sleigh to warm his feet. As soon as I spotted this, I tried to get him back into the sleigh, but it was too late. One of the sharp little kids noticed him walking and said, "That's not Santa Claus. That's John the mailman. I can tell by his walk."

That was the atmosphere Joe entered when he visited me at the parish. The people there loved him. And Joe loved coming there. We had a lot more potential for fun than at my other parish, in Scotia, where I had been only an assistant. At Mount Carmel I was pastor and felt freer to take the time to play, so we had a good time together.

Usually, I would bring Joe or Pete up with me after we finished supper at his folks' house. When Joe came along, he would ask on the way, "Fahd, are we going to have a party tonight?"

"We sure are, Joe. As soon as we get there and you get ready for bed."

Our party consisted of a piece of pie or cookies and an ice cream soda. When we finished, I brought him upstairs and tucked him in to his bed, then said his prayers with him. Usually, I would tell him a story with a little lesson and he would fall off to sleep. (He no longer had any nighttime mishaps at this point). As I still had work to do, I would go back downstairs and work until I was tired. It was fun having Joe at the house. He was never demanding, though I knew he wished I would spend more time with him. His life was to a great extent fantasy. He had the rare ability to mix fantasy with real life, and to enrich his life with his dreams. I think he lived his whole life that way.

One day after Mass and breakfast, we took a walk across the highway to explore the woods. It was a favorite spot for the parish maintenance men to look for bear's beard mushrooms. Well, Joe wasn't interested in mushrooms, but discovered a huge culvert, eight feet in diameter, that went under the thruway. When Joe asked what it was, I told him it was just a big drainpipe to conduct water under the highway. He had never seen anything so huge and was intrigued by it.

I don't know how he made the transition, but he burst out with a great idea: "Fahd, this is a great place to play cops and robbers." So we played cops and robbers for the next hour, something I had not done in over thirty years. I felt sort of foolish, as my ability to fantasize had long since vanished and all I could see was muddy water, an old culvert full of cobwebs, dirt all over my good shoes and pants—but no cops and no robbers. To Joe, however, it was the climax of a real adventure, lived out with all the excitement of a TV thriller. On the way back to the rectory, Joe walked beside me full of mud and looked up at me and said, "Fahd, wasn't that a lot of fun?"

"It sure was, Joe," I responded with evident enthusiasm.

"Can we go back up there again, Fahd?"

"I'm sure we will, Joe."

Fortunately, I had a long-suffering housekeeper named Lena Brignole. She was the one who did most of the work preparing for Santa Claus's annual tour through the village. She was also a mother to Joey and Pete when they came to visit. She would prepare little snacks for them, and on chilly days, a dish of chicken soup, which I could hear them slurping all the way upstairs. Their dirty clothes she would put in the washing machine and have all ready when it was time for them to go home.

As much fun as Joe had while playing, he was a different person when we were at morning Mass. He would sometimes serve the Mass or just sit at the side, deep in thought. Even as a child, he had a sensitive, serious side to his personality, a certain reserve that was very difficult to penetrate. After receiving Communion, he would go back to his place and kneel. He would never talk about what he was thinking, but somehow I knew he was very close to Jesus during those few precious moments. I would have loved to know his thoughts, but whenever I asked questions, he would just smile and say nothing. I soon learned not to pry.

Occasionally when Joe and Pete came to visit and I would be unable to spend much time with them, I would ask my secretary's daughter, Diane, if she would babysit, especially at night if I had to go to a wake. (I felt it might be too much for them to see a corpse at so young an age, though I now realize it is such a common experience in these times that it probably would not have shocked them.) It bothered Joey terribly when I left him, and he showed it by being really nasty to Diane. I could never fully understand why he was so upset. I guess it just made him feel bad that I would cut him out of a part of my life. Joe was unusually sensitive, and when his feelings were hurt, he could become quiet and moody.

I'll never forget one episode. It occurred when we were returning to his house after a few days at the rectory. It was a Sunday. Masses were over. As we were driving back to Schenectady, he picked up the electronic garage opener and began talking to a kid named Mack.

I asked him, "Joe, who are you talking to."

"Mack."

"Who's Mack?"

"My friend."

"How come you never told me about him?"

"I just met him."

"Where?"

"Around."

"Is he a nice kid?"

"Yes."

"Does he talk back to you when you talk to him on that thing?"

"Of course he does, Fahd."

"May I talk to him?"

"Yes, if you like." Handing me the gadget, he said, "I don't think he will talk to you, Fahd."

"Why, Joe?"

"Because he was told not to talk to strangers. Besides that, he's shy. He only talks to me."

This was all said with complete seriousness. It was just a game he played, one that went on for months, whenever he came to Amsterdam. It wasn't that he was lonely or lacked friends. Joe was one of the most popular boys in school and had many friends. But he liked to play imaginary games.

I was a little concerned about his talking to Mack, so I tried to distract him by taking off my watch and letting him wear it. He was so happy and wore it so proudly. Later on, after we had arrived at his house and finished dinner, I asked him for the watch. He gave it back but looked so sad, and wouldn't even say good-bye to me when I left. I felt terrible, though I probably should have understood. That incident bothered me for years. Apparently it bothered him, too, because just a little over a year ago he brought up the incident.

"Fahd, remember the time you gave me your watch and then took it back?"

"Yes, I've thought of it so many times."

"So did I."

"Why did you get so mad?"

"Because I thought that when you gave me the watch you liked me, and when you took it back you didn't like me."

"Oh, Joe, you know I've always loved you. How could you ever think I didn't love you?"

"I don't know. I guess I was just hoping I could have something that belonged to you. I've never forgotten that incident, Fahd."

"Neither have I, Joe. But now you know I have always loved you."

"I know. It's great. It's like I have two fathers. When one gets mad at me, I always have the other one who isn't mad at me."

Around the time Joe was visiting me in Amsterdam, he began giving everyone in his family and all his friends nicknames in a fantasy language he had invented. It was not gibberish, though it would have been impossible to spell some of the words with our limited alphabet. The language was logically constructed and the vocabulary consistent. At first people thought it was funny, but since Joe insisted on speaking it for the next sixteen or seventeen years, it finally drove everyone to distraction. Even Justice, the family's golden retriever, had a nickname. That dog was special to Joe. When he came home for lunch, he would spend most of the time playing with Justy, who would always respond when Joe called him by his nickname. The two had a special bond.

Hockey was the big thing in town in those days. A local architect named Gregory Crozier had earned his way through Rensselaer Polytechnic Institute in Troy by playing hockey. He had come from Canada and hockey was in his blood. His great ambition was to get the local kids interested. All the Della Ratta boys started in the Schenectady youth hockey league at an early age. Joey was five or six when he started. He was good. He switched between playing goalie and forward. Once, his team was up against a powerful Canadian squad. Until the last few minutes the score was o–o. Then Joey got a goal, the only one of the game, and his team won.

In school Joe was popular with both boys and girls, though he had a special feeling for, and would befriend, kids who were not accepted by others, particularly those with handicaps. Because he was such a warm and beautiful boy, many of the girls were in love with him. One, particularly, Joe really liked. Her name was Shannon Allen. One day Joey wrote her a little letter and put it on her desk. It started out, "I love you. Do you love me?" She turned to him and said, "No, you hit me all the time." They then started bickering, which caught the attention of Sally Van Schaik, the teacher. She asked Joey what was going on and he said, "Shannon is making fun of my stuttering." Shannon's jaw dropped. "I never said that," she told the teacher, but to no avail. Sally Van Schaik believed Joey and made Shannon get up in front of the class and apologize, while Joey sat there with a big smirk on his face. But the incident never marred their beautiful friendship, which continued through the years. In fact, it was from Shannon we got the story.

Sally Van Schaik, a friend of mine, and I were

talking about Joey one evening. She'd had him in the third or fourth grade. "As overactive as he was, I couldn't help but love that boy. Those big, sparkling brown eyes. The happy smile. But to get him to develop his academic potential without jumping all over him was a task. I tried everything.

"I tried rewarding him, then the other students expected rewards. I decided to give them bottle caps whenever they did a good job. I used to pick up bagsful of them at the convenience store. One day I ran out of them and told the class, 'Well, today, you are going to have to be good on your own. I have run out of bottle caps.' No sooner did I finish than Joey came up to my desk with a brown paper bag. I opened it. It was full of bottle caps.

"Joey was an excellent piano player even at that young age. I told him that if he was good during the day, I would let him play the piano during the last period. That did the trick. Practically every day he would play the piano, real lively music, not the kind he learned in music class, but the kind the kids liked. It was a treat for all of us, even myself.

"Another incident I remember involved an assignment I gave Joe, to write a story about one of his hockey games. I told him to mention the name of his team. Well, he wrote this nice little story and at the end wrote the name of the team. It was spelled like this: S-u-n-z-a V-i-t-t-l-i. I said to myself, 'What a funny name!' Later on it dawned on me what it meant. His coach had told the kids the name, but never spelled it out. The team was named after their sponsor, the Sons of Italy. I still laugh when I think of it.

"Joey was such a free spirit, so happy, and oh so active, but I couldn't help but adore that boy."

Early on, Joey was placed in a special program for children with unusual artistic talent. The school principal, Laura Vonie, loved Joey and insisted on his being selected. She and I had been friends ever since our involvement in a community crisis a few years before. It was at the time of the riot at Attica Prison. We decided to offer ourselves as hostages to avoid bloodshed during the standoff. It proved to be too late, as the governor ordered the National Guard to storm the prison that very day, with frightful loss of life. Laura and I were both devastated. I always re-member her as a remarkable woman, with extraordi-nary sensitivity to people. She had an uncanny ability to pick out a child's worth. She spotted Joey's talent immediately and wanted him in that special program. Being singled out helped Joey see himself in a better light, and he proved himself worthy of the choice. He was good in drama and was given key roles in many of the school plays, especially those involving music.

Joey was, of course, a free spirit and always followed the beat of a different drummer. Shannon Allen's brother Pat tells how Joey disliked gym class; in lieu of it, he and others were allowed to march around the ballfield, Joey playing his trumpet while he marched. But when it came to baseball, it was a different story.

One day when he came up to Amsterdam, he asked me if I would teach him how to hit a baseball. I showed him, we practiced for a while, then he finally caught on. When I threw the next pitch, it came back at me like a cannonball. After that, practically every pitch I threw he hit, and hit hard. He was a natural. Right after that, he signed up for Little League. He couldn't wait for practice. Tony Verteramo, Joey's coach, said he could hit a ball a mile, and encouraged him to keep playing. And he could run like a deer. He loved baseball.

His music teacher at the time was Mrs. Rice. She was a lovable woman who had patiently nurtured many budding musicians, including all the Della Ratta boys, so Joey was well prepared when he graduated to Mr. Hummel, his next piano teacher. Stanley Hummel was a tall, distinguished-looking man. I myself thoroughly enjoyed not only his exquisite piano renditions but just watching him walk across the stage. He was impressive! He in turn enjoyed watching Joey, with his baseball cap and glove, arrive on his bike for weekly piano lessons.

After each lesson Joey couldn't wait to get to his baseball practice. As time went on, Mr. Hummel became discouraged. Although he liked Joey, he knew he was more interested in baseball and other kid stuff at that point in his life, so he told Richard and Liz that the piano lessons were almost a waste of time.

Joe's balanced outlook, his varied interests, were a healthy expression of the joy he found in life. He had a zest for it, an appreciation for what was really important that revealed the inner beauty of his young soul. He never had any money. It was not important to him. He liked nice clothes, but never had the money to buy any. The taste was there, and everyone knew it, so at times we all made it possible for him to indulge . . . a little bit. And when he dressed up, did he ever look sharp! Even as a young boy.

Richard and Elizabeth insisted the boys learn to ski when they were young. John was a daredevil and would try the most dangerous trails. Michael and Rick also excelled, and still ski every chance they get. Joey, too, was a good skier, though I don't remember him having the passion for the sport that the others did.

A skiing incident I well remember occurred during a trip we all took to the Trapp Family Lodge. It was bitterly cold, and the roads through Vermont in those days were not very hospitable. We arrived in the early evening and had dinner in the old lodge. We sat before the fire, and the atmosphere was in the grand old Austrian Alps style—warm and cozy. Rather than individual rooms, there were big family rooms where groups slept together. It was fun. It made no difference anyway: we were so tired from the trip that we slept like mummies and were not wakened even by Richard's snoring.

Getting everyone moving next morning was a gigantic undertaking. After breakfast there was a bit of a logistics problem. The Trapp Family resort is designed for cross-country skiing. The Della Rattas wanted to down-hill. As I didn't ski, little Peter and I were odd men out. I told Richard and Elizabeth to go on their own and I would take care of Pete. That's how we ended up.

Pete was always restless and easily became bored. And when he did, he could be an itch. I got the bright idea of teaching him how to cross-country ski. At the time, Pete was only a year and a half old, or at most two years. As I was debating whether he was too young and could possibly be hurt, Maria von Trapp happened to walk by. We chatted for a while. She was most gracious. I asked her how she liked the musical and the movie based on her life. With a half smile and half-raised eyebrows, she said, "Well, it was a nice movie, but it really wasn't me. Look at me, do I look like Julie Andrews?" Maria was a large woman and not quite as pretty as Julie Andrews.

"Are you going skiing?" she asked us.

"I don't know. Don't you think he's a little too young?"

"No, no. Not at all. That's the age when children should learn to ski. That's when we learned back home. Go ahead and have fun. It's a good day for it."

She was right. So we went over to the shop, were fitted for skis and started out.

Peter did not do badly at all. We skied for about a half mile, and he shuffled along like a trooper, though it was cold, really cold. I felt a little sorry for him, as his cheeks were like two ripe tomatoes, and his nose like a cherry. Finally he gave up and said, "Fahdy, no skion. No skion, Fahdy."

Even I was a little tired. So we sat down under a tall pine tree and in thirty seconds he was sound asleep. I sat there looking across the fields just daydreaming as the snow fell. It was a perfect winter day, one of those days you dream about for Christmastime. It was quiet and serene. Nothing stirred but the pine needles on the trees around us.

Peter slept for almost an hour, then I woke him up and we started back. He wouldn't put the skis on again no matter how hard I tried to persuade him. "No skion, Fahdy." And that was that. I carried his skis back to the shop as he trudged along beside me. Then we went to the lodge dining room and had a bowl of chicken soup, and just wandered around until Richard and Elizabeth came back with the boys a couple of hours later. It was a good day. We finished it off with a delicious home-cooked meal, after which we started on our way back home, reminiscing all the way about *The Sound of Music* and the resemblance of the Van Trapps' interest in music to our own.

Three

WATCHING JOE GROW THROUGH THE YEARS was a
marvelous experience. He was full of fun and
his big brown eyes sparkled with mischief. He was
always playing tricks on people. But there was no real
malice or vindictiveness in him. Being sensitive, he
was easily hurt. Occasionally he would say, "I can't
understand it. Why would they want to do something
like that?" It was hard for him to understand how
people could be mean. The most he would ever do to
people if they hurt him was to hide something on
them, driving them to distraction until they found
whatever it was. As young as he was, his ability to

focus on spiritual things was extraordinary. He would make comments that made all of us stop and think. One day his father and mother and some of the family were sitting around talking, at one point about people running away from themselves and hiding their true selves from others. Joe had been listening. During a pause in the conversation, he came up with an interesting comment: "I know someone you can't hide from. That's God." I often wonder what was going through his mind when he said those words, or if he was hoping he could hide from something he had done.

Joe thought a lot about the suffering of innocent people. He found it difficult to understand why a God who is so kind should allow them to hurt so much, and why there is so much evil in the world. I tried to explain as best I could about evil and our kind God. It was difficult, however, as it is really a mystery.

Joe was hardly into third grade when he started showing interest in the trumpet. The interest grew, and although he was still taking piano lessons, his heart was no longer in them. His father had been a French horn player in the Albany Symphony Orchestra, and was delighted his son was leaning toward a wind instrument. I felt bad about it, knowing that Joey could have been an extraordinary concert pianist had he kept up his studies with Mr. Hummel. However, I felt it was not for me to persuade him to continue. I had always told him, once I realized the talent he had, that his music was his calling from God and he should follow wherever God was calling him. In a short time he was mastering the trumpet, and played fabulously. As difficult as it was for me to understand the kind of music he was playing, I could see he was well on his way to becoming a master at his craft.

At the time, I was still stationed at St. Joseph's in Scotia and had a good-size choir, about thirty adults in all, mostly singles and married couples. We met every week. At the Mass, during which the choir sang, the whole Della Ratta family was present, as well as the Taylor family; the kids sometimes came to the rehearsals as well. The Taylors and the Della Rattas were shining examples of how beautiful family life can be. The Della Rattas sang together. They prayed together. They celebrated life together.

And they vacationed together. I've already mentioned the skiing jaunt to Vermont. I'll never forget one summer when they decided to go on a cross-country trip in their station wagon. As I had taken my mother—and later on, both my parents—on vacation every year, I knew the country like the palm of my hand, so I was asked to go and be the navigator.

We went everywhere you could imagine, in less than a month. We visited Niagara Falls and Notre

Dame University, then passed through Springfield, Illinois, seeing the newly discovered log cabin village where Abraham Lincoln had lived and practiced as a young lawyer. It is a gem of a historical site and well worth visiting. Nearby is a natural amphitheater built into the adjacent field, where local people play period music and offer other entertainment of a historical nature.

Our prime objectives were the Grand Canyon, the Petrified Forest and the Painted Desert, as well as Bryce Canyon, Yellowstone and the redwood forests. The Grand Tetons were special, as was the Custer Battlefield National Monument, where we just meditated on the sadness of the terrible tragedy.

The Grand Canyon was a spectacular experience, though the kids wandered all over the place and we wasted time corralling everyone. At one point we were standing on the brink of the canyon. Johnny had strayed off somewhere, and when he finally spotted us, he came running excitedly down the incline, totally oblivious of the mile-deep drop in front of us. When I heard him coming I turned, and as I did, he slid on the gravel and ran into me, then almost collapsed when he saw the yawning chasm before him.

One of the trip's most fascinating sights, not just for the children but for the adults as well, was the cliff dwellings outside Colorado Springs. Storey built upon storey, not unlike our modern apartment complexes, provided both ventilation and protection from the elements. It was an extraordinary feat for a people who had no exposure to modern architecture or to traditional engineering principles.

Going from house to house, we had to climb ladders along the side of the cliff. Joey was only about four at the time and was terrified when he looked down and saw nothing beneath him for hundreds of feet. I told him to get in front of me and not to look back. He felt comfortable enough with that, so we walked up the ladder to the apartment above and then to the top of the cliff. The whole day was an exciting learning experience.

Although it is difficult traveling with children on vacation, the rough spots on this trip were minimal. Elizabeth had the foresight to bring along enough games to keep everyone busy during the long, monotonous rides. We also invented a traveling bingo game. We picked imaginary landmarks we might possibly run into, like a water tower or a gas station or a school. Whoever spotted one first got a point; the first one to amass five points won. It really was fun and kept the kids' minds off one another. The most remarkable feature of the trip was that the car held up, only once or twice needing minor repairs. The drive home did seem interminable—there was nothing that could match what we had already seen—but as the years pass, memories of that trip keep recurring, prompting a smile and happy thoughts.

$\mathcal{F}our$

J OE'S LIFE WITHIN BLOSSOMED EARLY. As he approached adolescence, I sensed a reserve and a certain sadness which I knew had always been there but which was becoming more prominent. I would ask him an offhand question, like how was he feeling, and he would just smile and say with a nod of his head, "Good, Fahd." That would be it. I could never get further. How I wish I could have! I knew there was a world of feelings floating around inside, feelings I sensed he couldn't process too well and was having difficulty dealing with. But it is so hard for young people to share, especially with adults. I guess it is a trait not limited to the young. Many people, and men particularly, have trouble talking about their innermost feelings. It is too bad, really. I don't know what prompts so many of us to keep our real, deepest selves so closely guarded. Our lives, as well as the lives of those we love, would be much richer if we all could share the things that mean most to us. I know that those thoughts and feelings may sometimes be dark and frightening, but isn't that the best part of love, sharing the fear and the pain, as well as the joys, the hopes and the dreams? It is one thing to perform touching symbolic deeds, but to describe what you feel inside—that is the real sharing of one's life. That was missing in Joe, and it hurt.

On the outside, all anyone could see was a happy, playful young fellow. I used to watch him closely, however, trying to understand what he was experiencing, trying to sense what was behind the sadness that seemed always to be lying just beneath the surface. At times I would get a glimpse.

It happened once when he was visiting Mount Carmel in Amsterdam. It was a few weeks before Christmas, and Joe and Pete (aged about ten and five, respectively) had come to make their presents. We had a fine ceramics program at the church, and this year Joe wanted to make a Nativity set. He picked the figures he wanted and sanded them carefully, then put them in the kiln. When they were ready, instead of glazing them, since we were short on time, he painted them in a creamy white, then highlighted them with a little color. This whole process took him quite a while. I was surprised at his patience. Every now and then I would stop over to the ceramics room to see how he was doing, and sit down and talk with him. I got to know him better at times like that, because when he was concentrating on his work, I could catch him off guard, he would talk a little more freely.

He told me, in one of those off-guard moments, that he was so glad to be able to *make* his Christmas presents. "They mean a lot more when you can make them, Fahd. I know I don't have any money, but even if I did, it is still a lot nicer to make things with your hands. It means more."

"You *don't* have much money, do you, Joe?"

"No, but that's all right," he said as he kept painting. "I don't need any anyway. I really don't care about money."

That little remark gave me a key to a corner of Joe's world and revealed much about what was happening inside. I knew he liked nice clothes. Money, however, was another matter. He never had any and it didn't matter. And yet he loved life. He loved baseball in the summertime and hockey in the wintertime. He loved skiing, which his family always did together.

He was a good runner (he was tall and had long legs). And he loved his music. But there was a natural detachment from material things that was refreshing, even if it was in a way disturbing, since it led to a most impractical lifestyle. And Joe *was* frighteningly impractical. His brothers, especially Michael and Peter, could fix anything. But Joe—you could give him a hammer and nails and he would have a difficult time figuring out what to do with them. Chances are he would hit his fingers more often than the nails.

Peter, Joe's younger brother, was just the opposite. Pete was unusually practical. He also had a keen interest in money, even as a child. I remember him putting whatever anyone gave him in a bank he kept in his room. It was surprising how much he saved in the course of a year. But even though he liked to save money, he was also generous with it. A few days before Christmas one year, he asked if I would take him shopping. When I asked why, he said he wanted to get presents for everybody and didn't want anyone to know about it, so it could be a surprise.

We went shopping. He did get presents for everyone, and I was shocked at the shrewd way he went about it. I asked how he knew which presents to buy and he said he had been listening to family conversations and heard people talking about what they liked. "So, I knew just what to get."

After he paid the salesman, I noticed him putting some money on the counter. As we walked away, I asked, "What was that about, Pete?"

"The girl after me didn't have enough money to pay for what she bought. The man was going to take them back. So I put on the counter what she needed."

"That was really nice of you, Pete. You are a good boy."

One time when the Della Rattas were visiting me—it was also around Christmas—some of my family were there: my brother Eddie; his wife, Kathleen; and their seven children. The rectory had never seen such life. It was snowing outside, so we decided to do some sledding. The only place we could go was across the highway where Joe and I played "cops and robbers." It was not a particularly good place, but when it was all you had, you made the best of it. I had built a sled for Pete when he was a baby—by this time he was perhaps a year and a half old—and someone now sent him down the hill in it. His mother happened to be at the bottom. Afraid that Pete would be hurt, she caught the sled as it hurtled toward her. But it was going so fast that the abrupt stop threw Pete over Elizabeth's shoulder and headfirst into a snowbank. Just his feet were sticking out. He looked so funny. Thank God he wasn't hurt. When we pulled him out, there was snow all over him. Totally unperturbed, Pete just stuck out his lower lip and blew the snow off his nose and eyebrows, and merely said, "Fun, again." Afterward, Joe pushed Pete around in a wheelbarrow, which was safer. Our two families together had a really good time that day.

When I was stationed at St. Joseph's in Scotia, we didn't have an organist and I talked Elizabeth into taking the job. She was also in the choir I started, along with Richard. Although I didn't know much about music, I directed. The first year we started learning Puccini's *Messa di Gloria*, which had just been discovered. He composed the work when he was only a teenager after his mother had told him how ashamed she was that with all his talent he had not written anything for God. Hurt by her comment, he sat down and composed this beautiful Mass. The "Gloria" is so lively that whenever we practiced it, the choir would end up dancing to the melody.

After I was transferred to Amsterdam, Elizabeth thought she might give up playing for the choir because Richard had night court and was unable to watch the kids. I made a deal with her, that if she continued on as organist, I would act as babysitter. She accepted the offer, and for the next four years I babysat on Thursday nights for Johnny, Joey and Pete. I didn't mind it at all. I had known the boys since they were infants, and I knew it would be fun.

The kids were thrilled when they found out I was coming. They were almost always on their good behavior. After supper they played for a while, and when it was time for bed, I would call them into the living room and we'd all plop down on the sofa or lie on the floor before the fireplace, and I'd tell them stories, which I made up for the occasion, each with a moral based on the children's conduct. One they all remember was a story about a little Chinese boy named Jo-Jon-Fun-Lo, who was terribly bored at home and wanted some excitement in his life. Late one day when his parents were working, he slipped out of the house and walked down to the wharf to see what was happening there. It turned out he was kidnapped and brought aboard a ship that was about to set sail. And on the story went. Needless to say, it ended well. There were hundreds of other stories. Every now and then the boys reminisce about those stories. They remember them as clearly as the night they first heard them. I've forgotten most of them. I suppose at the time that I was merely refining my storytelling ability. As active as the boys were, when I told them stories they lay there in rapt attention. Afterward they would go up to bed with no trouble, and I'd say prayers with each of them, and in no time they would be sound asleep. With a sigh of relief I would go down to the living room and fall asleep while creating fantasies out of the flames in the fireplace.

Then in 1978 I found myself without a parish. I was gone from Our Lady of Mount Carmel, where Joe and Pete had spent so many happy times. I never realized the effect this had on Joe, particularly, nor did I fully understand how much I really meant to him as a child. He told me years later how angry he was at the bishop for transferring me. It probably seemed to him as if the bishop had fired me. In his unusual sensitivity to others, Joe may have sensed the discouragement I was experiencing at the time.

It was a very difficult period in my life. The bishop had merged my parish with two others and had never got around to giving the three pastors new assignments. Totally disheartened, one of them took a job in a brickyard. Another just drifted until he finally got another parish. I was told to pick my own assignment. I applied for the position of campus minister at Rensselaer Polytechnic Institute. I heard nothing for almost three months. The bishop, initially surprised that the campus committee hadn't contacted me, later told me they had picked someone else. He then said they considered me too old to work with young people. That hurt. I was only forty-nine at the time. After that discussion, since there were no prospects for an assignment, I decided to take my mom and dad on a surprise vacation to the Grand Tetons. It was their fiftieth wedding anniversary. We spent a month out in Jackson, Wyoming, and had a wonderful time. The scenery was magnificent, the climate ideal (80 degrees during the day and 60 at night, with 2 percent humidity). We walked and drove for miles each day visiting the beautiful sights. One morning we took a fifteen-mile raft ride down the Snake River. What we saw at sunrise along the river was sheer poetry—animals and birds of every description watering themselves in the quiet of the breaking dawn.

My mother and father enjoyed a much-needed rest on that vacation. Most days I rose early while they slept, and took a walk into the mountains to think and pray. I sensed my bishop felt uncomfortable with me. I had always been outspoken with the previous bishop when I felt strongly about something, though I helped out the present one in difficult predicaments, for which he said he was grateful and really owed me. But for some reason he didn't seem concerned about what I was going through or to care whether I was assigned or not. I may have been wrong. I am sure he had many other things on his mind. However, my priesthood was too important to me to let go of that easily.

I felt certain my parents never sensed how deep my pain was. I didn't want it to cloud the joy they were experiencing on their second honeymoon. It gave me profound pleasure to see them walking along together on the mountain trails holding hands and drinking in all the breathtaking sights. I intentionally walked way ahead of them so that they could have some privacy to share thoughts and feelings, which they never really had a chance to do back home.

A rather fascinating thing happened during that vacation. Michael Della Ratta and some friends had left on a hiking trip through the Tetons, organized and led by Bill Allen, a YMCA counselor. I found out where they were supposed to be and tracked them down. They got the shock of their lives when we came upon them deep in the woods.

"How did you ever find us, Fahd?" Michael asked, still in shock.

"Oh, I was always a good tracker. We thought you might need some good food, so we stopped and loaded up with enough supplies to last until the end of your trip."

"Gee, that's great, Fahd! All we've had to eat

was freeze-dried food for the past two weeks while we were hiking."

My mom and dad got a huge thrill finding the kids way out in the middle of nowhere. They liked the Della Ratta boys. They were so wholesome and always respectful.

Joey also went on Bill Allen's trips. Once, he flew to Arizona, where he was supposed to meet Bill at the airport. When he didn't show up, Bill called his parents to find out if he'd caught his plane. Everyone was on the verge of panic until Joey responded to a call on the airport sound system and came over to greet Bill. Joey had become so engrossed in a one-armed bandit that he forgot all about Bill Allen. The rest of the trip went well. Such hikes were hard for Joey, especially one to Mount McKinley, but he later recalled many times how breathtaking the views were from the mountain peaks. I am sure Joey had wonderful spiritual experiences during those ecstatic moments. He spoke of them so often.

After our Grand Tetons vacation my parents and I drove back to New York. I was pretty much on my own, with no place to live. It was awkward for a forty-nine-year-old priest to have to ask his mother and father if he could move back home because he didn't have an assignment. I think Joey sensed what I was going through. He was extraordinarily perceptive. He told me how devastated he was when I had to leave Mount Carmel. Perhaps this was not only because he sensed my pain but also because he had so many beautiful memories of the parish that he felt were being closed off from him forever. I knew he was hurting for some reason, but he wouldn't talk about it. He hinted he was angry at the bishop but gave me no reason. All I said to him was, "Oh, Joe, you can't let these things bother you. I've been transferred many times. God always ends up putting us where he wants us, and each time it opens doors to a new adventure, so don't feel bad."

I did finally get an assignment, one that was taking the bishop quite some time to fill. It was St. Patrick's, a little village parish that covered a territory ten miles long and almost ten miles wide. The church itself was a quaint brick building of the type you see on Christmas cards. I was there only two weeks when a delegation representing eight hundred parishioners and other local people asked to see me, demanding to know where I stood with regard to a housing project the diocese was planning. The bishop had said nothing to me about this when he asked me to take the assignment, so I was caught totally off guard. The delegation went on to tell me that for two years diocesan officials had been planning a major housing project for migrant farmers at the local mushroom plant and had never approached the town officials (who were either on the parish council or trustees of the parish). The project was slated for a neighborhood where there were seventeenth- and eighteenth-century homes, one of them belonging to a member of the Pillsbury family. Only with God's help and with my own sensitivity to the people's concerns was I able to heal wounds caused by their conflict with the bishop, to renew the people's spirit and to keep them in the Church. They were a wonderful, faithful congregation, and during the short time I was there, we ended up becoming good friends and accomplished many worthwhile projects together, having a lot of fun in the process. During those two years at St. Patrick's before my health broke, I was able, with the help of the loyal parishioners, to get the parish back on its feet. I still have fond memories of that brief interlude in my life and of the many friends who have kept in touch.

Five

IN MIDDLE SCHOOL, Joe began to blossom. His sunny personality brightened all lives, even the teachers'. It was easy to overlook his impetuosity and exuberance. He was so innocent and lovable. He radiated such happiness and real interest in people that even if they were depressed when they approached him, they would walk away smiling, knowing someone cared for them. Even though this was a natural expression of Joe's personality, the question always in the back of his mind was: "How would Jesus want me to treat people?"

There were more plays and musicals put on in

middle school, and Joe shined in these activities. He was a born actor. When he played Hawkeye in M*A*S*H, I remember being shocked at how far he had come from the little boy I had known. He also played the part of Ralph Rackstraw in H.M.S. *Pinafore*. In the stage band concerts, he played flügelhorn solos, doing an exceptionally good job with "Yesterday" by Paul McCartney and John Lennon. In the summer of that same year, 1983, he received a 6 A+ rating for his New York State School Music Association solo, the highest rating at the most difficult level for high school students, and Joe was only in middle school. Even Dr. Campbell, the director of the association, expressed his pride in Joe's ability, and how much he enjoyed playing with him. During all these accolades, one trait stood out dramatically: Joe's humility. He never became proud or haughty. He just loved music and enjoyed making people happy when he played. I don't think he realized how good he was.

While Joe's middle school years were happy ones, high school brought heartbreak for him and everyone else. After his first year, his parents decided it would be better for him to move from Linton to a private school. So they arranged to send him to Albany Academy, which had an excellent reputation for academics and for the personal attention given to students. The move did not turn out well. The school was far away and was not easy to get to. Joe's parents found a student at the academy who lived in Schenectady and whose parents agreed to have their son pick up Joe and drive him to and from school. The whole experience was a disaster. The boy resented being saddled with Joe every day and treated him terribly. Humiliated, Joe retaliated by puncturing the tires of the boy's car, which created an unpleasant situation for both sets of parents. Soon after the incident Joe was back at Linton.

If the situation was bad before, it was worse now. Albany Academy had insisted that Joe repeat his previous year, so the time spent there put him a year behind his former classmates. Some of the teachers weren't particularly happy about having to take him back. They could never get used to anyone like him. A free spirit can be threatening to a person who may be insecure in his or her own position, as in the case of one teacher, who apparently felt intimidated by Joe's extraordinary talent. How does a teacher handle someone who is so different? And Joe *was* different. The only person comparable to Joey I can think of is Mr. Blue, the fictitious character in the book of the same name by Myles Connolly, the mentor of the famous movie director Frank Capra. There are many similarities between the two. Joe's life also reminds me of Francis Thompson's *The Hound of Heaven*.

Not understanding Joe's personality, someone started the rumor he was on drugs. His parents had him tested and the doctor certified he was clean. It broke Joe's heart to be treated so shamefully. The worst of it was that some of the teachers and administrators treated him as if he *were* on drugs. He started to become depressed. In his schoolwork, which was always difficult for him, he began to fail miserably. He would try hard to do well, though perhaps not hard enough. One teacher in particular he wanted so much to please. He really loved her. But even in her subject he did poorly, and this with his best effort. Week after week he came home with poor marks. He grew discouraged. His parents prodded him to do better, which made him even more discouraged. I felt bad for him because I could see his pain and dejection but could do nothing about them.

One day I told him that his music was what was important and that that was his calling from God. "Music is your vocation, Joe, don't compromise it for anything. Your music is God's gift to you to be nurtured and treasured."

I don't know whether that was the right thing to have said to him, but a short time later, when his music was in jeopardy and he had to make a decision, he remembered those words and acted on them.

It happened while he was in the Empire State Youth Orchestra, a highly prestigious appointment for a young student. Joe often played solo with the orchestra, the conductor thinking very highly of him and his ability. Around the same time, he was scheduled to make his Confirmation at his local parish church. However, there was a conflict in schedules. Joe's Youth Orchestra rehearsals were on Tuesday nights, and Confirmation classes were on Tuesday as well as on Monday nights, though ordinarily the students had an option. Joe asked the person in charge if he could attend the Monday night classes, but he was told, "No, this is one of those times in your life when you have to make a decision as to what is important." It was an inane remark and Joe was crushed; he was so looking forward to his Confirmation. It would be the day when he finally made his mature, lifetime commitment to Jesus. That meant a lot to him. It was a difficult crisis because he knew his music was important to God. Many young boys would have just given up religion in the face of such official insensitivity. But for Joe, Jesus was his best friend and he would figure out his own way to make his personal commitment. So, on his own, he found a priest who was really Christ-like and sensible and who immediately understood Joe's struggle. His name was Father John Provost. He was pastor of St. John the Evangelist Church, which was not far from Joe's house, and he was only too happy to allow Joe to prepare for his Confirmation at his parish. When the day came, I was honored that Joe asked me to be his sponsor. It was a happy day in Joe's life.

Joe's Confirmation came at a time when he needed this added reinforcement. Adolescence is painful, and although there are joys in abundance at the new life coursing through a teenager's body and soul, there are also self-doubt and confusion, as well as feelings of guilt over not having the strength to live up to ideals. The dreams are bright and shining, the weaknesses glaring and humbling. No one is immune from them. I think one of the great difficulties for teenagers is that they expect too much of themselves, and so do parents and teachers. We so easily forget that adolescence is a time of breaking away—from the past, from parents, from things learned in child-hood—so that boys and girls can establish their own identity and individuality as people. That is not easy. It is not that teenagers reject everything taught by parents; rather, they need to validate what they have learned, to accept and embrace it as their own. They no longer want to feel, "I am what my parents want me to be." They want to be able to feel, "I am unique.

I am special. I am myself." It is the way God made us. We have to be ourselves.

Many parents have an extremely difficult time accepting this process. They look upon it as a rejection of all they hold sacred. Sometimes they pressure and badger their children to carry on their own dreams and ideals, and when it doesn't happen, the punishment—often emotional—can be harsh and swift, like a judgment from God. That is a sure way to destroy a child, by not allowing him or her to have an independent life.

Fortunately, Joe's parents were not like this. They allowed their children from their early years to express themselves. At times, this could be unnerving, and the kids got into plenty of mischief, but when they grew older, their lives stabilized and showed none of the instability and heartrending self-searching that characterize so many grown-ups today. They were allowed to be children when they were children, and when they grew up, they had got their childhood out of their system, which is the bottom line of good mental and emotional health.

But Joe was always a free spirit. One time when I went over to the Della Rattas', I heard a trumpet playing. I went inside, but found no one. I called, but no answer. After a while I decided to leave. Going out the front door, I could hear the trumpet louder than ever. I looked up and there was Joe, sitting on the peak of the roof, playing his heart out. There he could feel free as the breeze floating past. I later found out he had brought several eggs and was throwing them down on top of a police car parked in the street. Joe didn't like too many policemen. He had seen what some of them had done to certain friends of his, and felt that a lot of them were just mean and sadistic. The cop kept getting out of his car, trying to see where the eggs were coming from, and Joe just kept playing away on the trumpet as if he were totally unaware of what was going on.

At times Joe would come home from school with friends. One was a tall black boy with a husky build. Joe was teaching him how to play the piano. When I asked who his new friend was, he said, "A boy from Hamilton Hill. He would love to play the piano, but has no money, so I told him I would give him lessons." On other occasions he brought home friends who had reputations for getting into trouble. When asked why he hung around with those kids, he merely said, "Because Jesus would want me to. They have problems. And didn't Jesus hang around with people who had problems?" When I mentioned that he could get into trouble himself by associating with those kids, he replied, "Maybe that's part of it, Fahd. Didn't Jesus get into trouble?"

Joey

How do you answer that? I thought his answer was beautiful, but it also frightened me because it showed that his commitment to Jesus was uncompromising. And as friendly and caring as Joey was, he was not strong enough to be a leader. Lacking this, he was unprotected and vulnerable. He was just a gentle, playful boy who loved life. Whatever his friends wanted to do, that was good enough for him, within limits. He had a difficult time not being part of their fun, even if it sometimes got him into trouble.

Joe had no difficulty accepting people who were different. One summer during his high school years, he was hired to work at the hospital across the street from his house. He was responsible for keeping the psychiatric ward clean. Years afterward his supervisor, a woman with a wonderful sense of humor, told his parents about Joe's performance.

"The ward was always immaculate," she said. "I couldn't understand it, because I never really saw Joe doing any work. He spent most of the time chatting and joking with the patients. A couple of times I saw him asleep on one of the beds. I knew he stayed up late playing music with his friends, so I never said anything to him. But for the life of me, I couldn't figure out how he could do all the work so perfectly, until one day I finally got to the bottom of it. I found out that whenever he took a nap, the patients took his mop and bucket and dust rags and did all the work for him so that he wouldn't get into trouble. They really loved him. He was also good therapy for them. They knew he cared for them."

It was at about this time that the house next door to the Della Rattas' was sold to the state for a group home for the mentally handicapped. Some of the neighbors were irate. Joe's parents were concerned because they had been thinking of moving to a house large enough to also serve as Richard's law office, and were now afraid they couldn't get a fair price for their present home.

At the mention of selling the house, Joe's response was, "Sell our house? You'll never sell this house, and besides, God probably wants the group home next to us because he knows we're not NIMBYs, and we'll be kind to them."

"What's a NIMBY?" his mother asked him.

"You know, Mom, it's those people who are all for group homes, but Not In My Back Yard."

In school, Joe's difficulties persisted. As good as he was in music, he just could not make it academically. And yet he was not slow: he was just so totally focused on his music that he found it difficult to concentrate on anything else. Melodies were going through his head all day long. If only he could have concentrated on his music alone like great musicians of the past. He tried so hard to make the adjustments everyone demanded of him but just could not do it.

One night I was over at the Della Rattas' for supper. Joe was depressed. I could tell he was really down. His parents were on him for getting low marks. I told him, "Joe, do your best. If your marks are from doing your best, then be content with it. But make sure it's your best. Don't be too easy on yourself!"

When some of the others had left the room, he asked, "Fahd, do you think I'm stupid?"

"Why do you ask?"

"Because I try so hard and I keep failing. There is one teacher I like and I want so much to please her. I even fail her classes."

"No, Joe, you are not stupid. You are a genius. You can already see the happiness your music brings to people. One day you will bring joy to millions of people with your happy spirit and your music. The reason you are having trouble with your other subjects is because you shouldn't be taking them. The school should make provisions for students like you whose talents lie elsewhere, in fields other than academics. But do your best! That's all that God expects of you, Joe, and that's all that counts."

Then he told me something that frightened

me. "Fahd, you know this morning on the way to school, when I was walking past the hospital, I thought of going up on the roof and jumping off."

"Why would you want to do that?"

"Because there is this one teacher who is mean and I get so depressed the way she treats me. I hate to go to school. As I get closer and closer to school, I get more and more depressed."

"Joe, you are going to come across a lot of people who are mean. You can't let them affect your life. They have real problems, these people, and they get relief by being mean to others. When they see the hurt they inflict on others, they feel a certain morbid kind of relief. I know it's sick, but you can't let those kind of people affect you, Joe. It will make you sick."

I thought so many times about what Joe had said, and I began to realize how deeply sensitive he was, much more so than I had realized. His discouragement and depression were deepening, yet they showed only on rare occasions. On the surface he was his naturally happy self, and was happiest when he could make others happy. But the depression troubled me deeply. I wished I could have helped him more. I remembered the anguish I went through during the twelve years of my own depression when I was in the seminary. It was unrelenting and paralyzing.

I went home with a heavy heart that night. Joe's remark about his inability to do well in his academic subjects brought to mind a matter that had concerned me ever since my years as a teacher. I had had many high school students of average and below-average intelligence. They struggled so hard to understand more advanced subject matter, but in no way could they compete with the brighter students. The material was beyond their grasp. For the life of me I could not understand why the schools made these kids take these subjects, in many cases damaging them psychologically by humiliating them in front of their more gifted classmates. It didn't make sense. Yet these kids had talent. They were good at music, and art, and mechanics, and any of a wide range of subjects. These were the courses they should have been taking—courses that could have prepared them for life—while still studying the basic subjects they needed. As it was, when they finished high school, they were prepared for nothing, whereas the college-bound kids were all set. It is no wonder we have had so many problems with our young people: we have so frequently set them up for a hopeless future.

At one point in Joe's sophomore year, Richard and Elizabeth were called into the vice principal's office. He told them that Joe was unable to measure up and was being transferred to another school—a place where they just dumped kids the teachers no longer wanted to be bothered with. This school also had a very high percentage of students who were in serious trouble with the police. Further, there was no music program, no band, not even a choir. Richard and Elizabeth were furious and demanded that Joe be kept where he was. The vice principal refused, so they applied for a superintendent's hearing, at which they won Joe a reinstatement. All these episodes were shattering to Joe's opinion of himself.

Another shattering experience: suspension from school toward the end of the year for being late. While a student was on suspension, he or she was not allowed to participate in any extracurricular activities. One of those activities happened to be the annual concert at which Joe was scheduled to play the solos. The vice principal again refused to relent, even when the music teacher said she had no replacement. She ended up asking one of the faculty to play Joe's parts.

Not too long afterward, the vice principal himself became the subject of complaints, and not having tenure, he was asked to resign. A friend suggested he come to me for counseling. Knowing what he had done to Joey made it very difficult for me, but I was able to help him get through his crisis, and in the process subtly show him a different way of treating people.

The rest of the year Joe managed to survive and even get passing grades, which made it possible for him to move on to his junior year.

Six

IN THE SUMMERS, Joe went to the Eastern U.S. Music Camp, directed by Tom and Grace Brown. They knew Joe well. He had been going to their camp since seventh grade. Tom told me that even way back then Joe wanted to be the best and he played far beyond his grade level. He put his whole heart into his music and was very competitive. Each year he progressed dramatically, Tom said, and he knew that later on Joey would be able to get into any top music school and would take off like a rocket.

Tom and Grace had a profound impact on Joe's life. These two dedicated musicians understood him and were interested in him as a person. It made all the difference in the world, especially after the way he was treated at school. The teachers loved him, and his fellow musicians delighted in his playfulness and great humor, as well as in his lively trumpet playing. At the music camp he blossomed.

Sean Lowery, who taught Joe trumpet there, thought very highly of him, recognizing his potential from the start. "Joe had incredible talent and did not have to work hard to do well, and he knew it. It was frustrating to work with him—he wouldn't apply himself. He was in junior high then. He was always fun to listen to and to be with, but difficult to teach. Yet, as difficult as he was, it was hard to be angry with him because he always had that cherub smile.

"I tried to take him aside and encourage him to improve in his academics so he could be accepted into whatever college would be best for his trumpet training. I guess he did improve. He did get into Juilliard. He couldn't have done much better than that. I think it was Freddie Mills, the trumpet player in the Canadian Brass. He talked to Joe and took an interest in him, and that made the difference. From then on I could see the progress. But as frustrating as he could be sometimes, he was a joy, and the jewel in my crown."

I think that description pretty well sums up

what Joe was like. He always reminded me of the orchids in my house. When I nurtured them, they were gorgeous. When I ignored them and forgot to water them, they withered and died.

At the end of the sessions in August, Joe would spend time working for me. By then I had retired and was living in a bungalow owned by a friend, an undertaker. I had no income and almost no money for rent. Regina Chicorelli was kind enough to let me stay in a little house she owned outside Albany, on a back road across from a farm. I paid her what little I could afford, and as I earned more from the sale of my books, I kept increasing what I gave her each month. She was a saintly woman who helped countless people throughout her life. I was just one, and I'm glad I was able to help and support her after her husband died. *Joshua* came out while I was living in that house; I shipped out all the orders from there. It was a difficult job and I spent countless hours packing books and processing invoices. Joe used to come down from Schenectady in what free time he had and help me pack books and bring them to the post office.

"Fahd, do you see where this shipment is going?" he said to me one day as he sat on the floor packing a case of books.

"No, where is it going?"

"India. And the next ones are going to Africa

and Pakistan, and one to England. How do people find out about your books, Fahd? You don't advertise."

"I don't know. I guess people just pass them around to relatives and friends who live in different places around the world. They just seem to circulate by word of mouth."

"Fahd, did you ever think your books would become so popular?"

"No, I didn't, Joe."

"If people only knew how you live, they'd be shocked. You don't even have any furniture, except the table and chair you made, and only a couple of dishes. You really don't care, do you?"

"I don't know, Joe. I don't think about it. It's nice to have nice things, but I haven't had any money the past few years and I sort've got used to living this way. I don't need much, and besides, I spend most of my time writing. The only time I feel bad is when people come to visit and I have no place for them to sit down. Sometimes people come for counseling and I get embarrassed because I really don't keep the place too terribly neat, with boxes and books and papers scattered all over. But they don't come to see a nice house, Joe. They come because they are hurting and need help. As long as they leave healed or feeling better, I guess that's all that really matters."

"Fahd, do you like being a priest?"

"I love it, Joe. The strange thing is that I am more a priest now than when I was working in busy parishes. Bringing Jesus to a hurting world is the essence of what priesthood means, and I do that more now than ever. When I was working in parishes, I saved the same people week after week. Now my parish is rapidly becoming the whole world, reaching people of all different beliefs and with no belief. And it just happens with no effort. I don't even have to leave this little house and the message spreads. It's a mystery the way God works, Joe. So always be patient with yourself and with people. It is God who guides your life, if you let him. And when bad things happen and people try to hurt you, it really can't do any permanent damage. It's just painful, but God won't let anything get in the way of what he wants to accomplish with your life, so be patient and trust your Friend. He will always be by your side to guide you.

"When I was leaving my last parish, I got a retirement card from a Protestant lady who was a good friend. In the card, she congratulated me and wrote a little note telling me I was just beginning my work. My calling from now on, she wrote, was to rebuild the Church. I thought it rather strange, since I was so sick, and concerned that I didn't have much time left. In fact, when I was finishing *Joshua*, I had the strongest feeling that the only real purpose of my life was to write a portrait of Jesus, and that when it was finished, God would take me home. The lady's note was a shock, but it was one of those little evidences of God's masterful attention to the details of what's happening in our lives. So we never know, Joe, what unexpected twists God has in store for us. That's why we should always trust Him. He has only good things planned for us. The fun is watching His goodness unfold each day, like a kaleidoscope."

"Fahd, you're so simple. You don't even realize how much you mean to people, do you?"

"Joe, I guess I'm too tired to notice. I just have a job to do. Most of the time I'm so tired, I spend half the day resting. How can you feel proud when you are so weak? As long as I can help people get to know how beautiful Jesus is, that's all I care about, Joe. I just feel honored he uses me.

"And you are the same way, Joe. God has given you a rare talent, and you have kept your simplicity and your humility. Don't ever lose that, Joe. It is a beautiful trait in you."

"I try to be like you, Fahd. You've always been my best friend. Remember when you used to call me your 'little friend' and I would call you 'my biggie friend?' "

"I remember everything you said, Joe. You have always been very special."

Those rare moments with Joe were very revealing. Every now and then he would open up and share his thoughts. What I was able to see provided me with a rich insight into spirituality. Joe had a love for Jesus that was real. It was like St. Peter's love of Jesus, the kind that no one could ever doubt. But like St. Peter, Joe was frighteningly weak. I would never hold him up as a model for imitation, except in his love of Jesus. What I was beginning to see, however, was something extraordinary developing. Joe was wonderfully human, and not afraid or ashamed of his humanness. Take his relationships with girls, for example. Because he was so handsome, girls easily fell in love with him and called him regularly. They were always there when he played his music in public. I don't know when he had time to go on dates; it seemed he was always practicing, sometimes far into the night. One time his brother John was coming home late, and as he drove his car into the parking area in front of the house, he noticed a ladder in the alley, then saw a girl climbing up to Joe's room! One of the nice things about Joe's relationships with girls was that he did not use them. They were his friends, and these friendships lasted through the years. I think he must have had a difficult time knowing how to cope with his girlfriends. His music was everything to him.

Joe's genius for friendship was not limited to girls. Nor were his friendships just casual, passing episodes; they were genuine, lasting relationships, the depth of which we only gradually came to understand. We never realized, either, till much later on the extent of Joe's dedication. He was always there when a friend needed him.

One of Joe's friends was a pianist named Ian. He was extremely talented but very much alone. He liked to practice at night, but since his father was trying to sleep, this obviously didn't work out. So he would go to Joe's house and the pair would stay up very late practicing duets in the living room, where there was a piano. Joe's father, a musician himself, was used to after-hours jam sessions, so Joe's and Ian's playing didn't bother him.

When Joe was out of town, Ian had a difficult time finding a place to play. Then he learned he could get into Union College's Memorial Hall, where he would go and practice in the middle of the night. He did this for quite a while until a security guard caught him and arrested him for trespassing. Joe asked his father to represent Ian in court, which he did. He prevailed with the judge, who merely warned Ian that there were to be no repeat performances.

At the end of Joe's junior year, he had a rare opportunity to play at the New York State School

Joey

Music Association Directors' Conference. His dream was to appear with the All State Jazz Ensemble, which presented an annual series of concerts in the main ballroom of the Concord Hotel in the Catskill Mountains. It was a wonderful chance for Joe, so he applied. One of his teachers offered to send a recommendation to the association's board. Joe was thrilled, since such a recommendation was critical to his being accepted. A short time later a board member called the teacher and asked for the letter. But the teacher said she would give only verbal recommendation. She then commenced saying the most horrible things about Joe: that, among other things, he was on drugs, that he was a thief and could not be trusted. When the board member began to question her more in depth, she hung up. Fortunately, the board president, a fair and judicious woman by the name of Mrs. Sugar, said that since there was no evidence to support the allegations, and the person was unwilling to commit herself in writing, there was no reason to consider them as trustworthy. Joe passed his audition, his application was accepted, and after weeks of grueling rehearsals— during which he showed himself disciplined, trustworthy and highly professional—he played his solos with the All State Jazz Ensemble. In attendance were school administrators and teachers, as well as parents and musicians, from all across New York State. Mrs.

Sugar said afterward that accepting Joe into the orchestra was one of the most fortunate decisions she had ever made. She commented on what a talented young man he was.

Also that same year, Joe's parents had him visit an old friend, John Simonelli, with whom Richard had played French horn during high school and college years. John had gone on to play with the Philadelphia Orchestra, and was presently in the Toronto Symphony Orchestra.

So, off Joe went by train to Toronto. John, appreciating Joe's rare talent, immediately had him play for Larry Weeks, first trumpet with the Toronto Symphony, who took Joe to his home and gave him a private evaluation. Larry suggested that perhaps Joe should go to Interlaken for his senior year to better prepare himself for a good music college. John and Larry both offered to help Joe in whatever way they could.

Joe came back home with mixed feelings. He was elated by John and Larry's confidence in his ability, but in no way would he consider leaving home and friends and girlfriend for a private school that was so far away. That was not even discussable. However, the family did take John Simonelli's advice and contacted Phil Smith, first trumpet with the New York Philharmonic. Trying to get through to this world-class musician proved a near impossibility. But when they did, they were immediately struck by his honesty and sincerity. They were also impressed that he would take the time to hear their son, a total stranger.

"My schedule is such," he said, "that when I am not traveling with the orchestra, I like to spend as much time as possible with my family, and on weekends I play with the Salvation Army Band. As far as 'evaluating' your son, I try to stay away from that word, because the first time my playing was evaluated, I was told not to go into music. However, if you want to come to my house, I will hear your son play."

The family set a date and went to New Jersey to visit Phil Smith. When the lesson was over, Phil encouraged Joey to pursue his musical career and gave him the names of a couple of teachers at New York's Juilliard School with whom he could study during his last year in high school. Phil would not take a penny from the Della Rattas, no matter how much they insisted. They were deeply touched by the man's religious sensitivity, however, and on returning home, they sent him an autographed copy of *Joshua*.

Another old friend of Richard's from his days at Hartwick College was Fred Mills of the Canadian Brass. The family had stayed close to him over the years, and when he came to Schenectady to play, he would frequently spend the night with the Della Rattas. On those occasions he would give Joe music lessons and practical advice as well. Fred endeared himself to Joe. Sometimes after concerts Fred and Ron Romm would share their experiences with Richard and Joe and Liz over dinner.

That same summer Joe and his parents visited Fred in Toronto. Fred invited Joe to stay at his "pad," since he had the weekend free. Joe was thrilled. It was an unforgettable, mind-boggling experience for him—hearing *how* Fred practiced, practicing with him, learning from one of the best trumpeters in the field. Fred encouraged Joe, telling him he had what it took, but that he needed to be really dedicated, since only about one in four thousand make it to the top.

Fred also suggested, as did Phil Smith, that he take lessons from Mark Gould, first trumpet with the Metropolitan Opera. Joe took this advice and traveled to New York City periodically to meet with Mark. By the end of his senior year, there was a noticeable difference in Joe's playing, in his tone and in the way he practiced.

Those trips to New York, however, were not always smooth. One time Joe was distracted and missed his train stop and ended up in Harlem, where he walked the streets trying to find where Mark lived. A black cab driver noticed him walking by himself carrying his trumpet. He stopped his cab and called to Joe, "Boy, you're in the wrong part of town. Get in here and I'll take you where you're going." He told him never to do that again. It was too dangerous.

On another occasion Joe missed his train and was stuck in Grand Central Station. He had been too busy watching—and losing his money in—a shell game, the kind that one can find on any corner in the city. When he called home to tell his mother he might have to spend the night in Grand Central, she was frantic. She finally ended up calling Mark Gould, who sent a cab to pick up Joey and bring him to his apartment. He paid the bill and called Joe's parents to assure them their son was safe and sound.

These were relatively harmless events in Joe's life. The more hurtful ones I heard of only second-hand and usually after they happened. Thinking about them now, I can understand the pain that all these setbacks must have caused the boy's extremely sensitive soul, as well as the reason for the sadness in his eyes. Strangely, he would never talk about the hurtful things people did to him, and would never say bad things about the people themselves. All he would ever say when someone brought up various incidents was, "I can't understand why they would want to do something like that." There was nothing truly mean or vindictive in Joe's nature.

In fact, at Christmastime each year, people from the church that had refused to confirm Joe would call and ask him to play the trumpet at midnight Mass. This he did faithfully, even after he graduated and was home from Juilliard on Christmas break. His brothers asked him one night, "You mean, you are going to play over there after the way they treated you?" Joe's simple reply was, "I'm not playing for them. It's Jesus' birthday, and it's my present to him." That was all he would say, and that ended the discussion. There was nothing really petty in Joe's personality. Others of a less noble spirit would have left the Church when they were offended. But for Joe the Church was Jesus' gift to him, and he could understand that if church workers were un-Christ-like and insensitive, it offended Jesus more than himself. To have walked away would have made him feel like a Judas. His loyalty to the Church was solid and mature. That in itself was a testimony to the depth of his faith, surprising in a person so young.

Another thing Joe used to do during the Christmas season was play with the Alex Torres Latin Kings. They were, and still are, an excellent band. Joe loved Spanish music because it was so lively; it was a perfect vehicle for him. He would also appear at a local nightclub where people came just to hear him play. A retired musician was at Joe's gig one night. In the course of our conversation with him, he told us he kept an eye out for when Joe would be playing. "He's good, that boy!" the man said. Richard and Elizabeth beamed.

Seven

I N HIS SENIOR YEAR Joe applied to the Juilliard School of Music in New York City and went there for an audition. Only two trumpet players who tried out were accepted. Joe was one of them. He was beside himself with delight. The following fall he started classes, thrilled with the real beginning of his career, with his new friends and with the totally professional atmosphere. He was finally at home, and thriving.

Besides attending classes at Juilliard, Joe auditioned for the New York City Youth Orchestra and made first chair (there were three trumpeters in the orchestra). The orchestra rehearsed and played concerts in Carnegie Hall. The line for the Sunday concerts was sometimes two blocks long. New Yorkers loved to come and hear the young people play. Joe stayed with the orchestra for three years, highlighted by the centennial celebration of Carnegie Hall. This concert was nationally televised as "Carnegie—One Hundred" in 1991. At that concert Joe played both first trumpet and the solo trumpet part in *Pictures at an Exhibition*. That was a stunning accomplishment for a young, aspiring musician. It was a proud evening especially for his parents, since the program was widely acclaimed besides being on national television. Yet, even with this celebrity status, Joe still kept his simple humility. It was as if someone else had done the performance, with Joe just as a spectator. He said afterward to his parents, "How did you like the concert? Wasn't that a great concert? Didn't the violinist and So-and-so and So-and-so do a great job? You know, they are really great musicians and they're nice people, too." That was a good trait in Joe. He could not only recognize the talent in another musician, he could rejoice in it. And the beautiful part of it all was that it wasn't put on or contrived, but genuine, right from his heart.

Toward the end of his sophomore year, however, something happened at Juilliard. Joe didn't turn in a paper for one of his courses, which was critical to his passing and going on to his junior year. He was asked to take a year off to think things over and then apply all over again. He was devastated. He felt like a failure. Rather than coming home in triumph after a great year, he arrived ashamed and discouraged. He hoped Juilliard might relent and wrote to them. When the reply came in the mail, Joe read it, said nothing to his mother (who knew the letter had come) and went out into the backyard with Justy, the family's golden retriever. The two sat on the steps together as Joe cried his heart out, all the while hugging his loyal friend. His mother watched the two of them through the window and never forgot that touching scene.

Though Elizabeth and Richard were disappointed, they helped Joe through the crisis and encouraged him to take courses at the local community college so that he wouldn't fall behind. He applied to the college and signed up for two courses, as well as private trumpet lessons. He spent the year well and accomplished a lot.

That summer he worked at my house in Altamont, a village a few miles southwest of Schenectady. By that time, I had already written *Joshua* and it had become a national bestseller. I had moved from the bungalow to a place on a high hillside overlooking Altamont, which I intended to use for private, informal retreats. (As a thank you to Regina for her kindness during those difficult years, I painted an acrylic seascape for her living room.) The new place had spacious grounds, two ponds and extensive forests with mountain trails. This was the setting in which Joe worked when he was home on vacation. One summer he missed while he went on the road with the Glenn Miller Orchestra; part of another summer he played at the Berkshire Festival at Tanglewood, Massachusetts. Other years he worked on the grounds, helping the gardener.

The summer following his stint at the community college, he weeded the perennials and helped me prepare a plot for a vegetable garden. It was an impossible piece of ground, rocky and filled with heavy clay.

"Fahd," Joe said one day when he was ready to give up, "do you really think we can get things to grow in this stuff? Even the pick bounces off it. We've been working for days and all we have is just a few feet."

"Joe, it's like life. The most precious things are frequently the most painful. You can learn a lot from working in the earth. Be patient! Some day you will be proud of this little garden and you will wonder at what a little miracle it turned out to be."

"Fahd, the miracle will be if I don't break my back. I don't know, Fahd. With all the land you have here, there must be a better spot than this to plant your garden."

"Joe, this is one of the few places that gets sun all day. The growing season here is short, so we need all the sun we can get, especially with that mountain behind us. Don't give up, Joe. We'll have fun with it."

I spent some time with him, but he did most of the work himself. It took him the better part of a week to dig up the soil and clear away the rocks. I had a truckload of topsoil delivered, which he mixed in with the clay and worked it over and over until the earth was fairly consistent. The end result was a small plot, only about twenty-five feet along the front by about fifteen feet in from the driveway. We went down to the garden store and bought some tomato and pepper plants, plus a few eggplants and seed corn. We also picked up a few dozen strawberry plants. It was late in the season by the time we got to the store, and everything was pretty well picked over and dried out. The manager told us we could have the plants, as he wasn't too sure they were still alive. They did look as if they should be buried rather than planted. Joe laughed and said, "Fahd, I don't believe you. First, you ask me to dig a garden out of concrete, then you buy plants that are practically dead and you expect them to make it. Do you really think those things are going to live, especially in that soil?"

"Joe, as long as there's life, there's hope. Never give up."

We did plant them, and he watered them daily. Three weeks later they were strong and healthy and well on their way. The corn we had trouble with. The crows came at dawn. The scarecrow they looked at with utter contempt, and right under its feet they dug up each kernel, one by one. Every day we would plant more corn; every day the crows and then the squirrels would eat it. It was one continuous battle. I was tempted one day to shoot them, but I was too proud: that would have been an admission of defeat, an acknowledgment that my intelligence couldn't outwit them. I know this is totally out of context, but it is one of the reasons why I am against the death penalty. It is an expression of frustration and the ultimate abandonment of hope in someone God loves.

Our persistence did pay off and by the end of the summer we harvested at least two bushels of tomatoes, not too many peppers and maybe a few dozen ears of delicious white corn. We got bushels of squash from some seeds I had scattered during the winter. Joe was able to bring home several bags of squash flowers for his mother to dip in batter and deep-fry. The strawberries had to wait until the next year.

That was a good summer. Joe was his happy, playful self. He enjoyed the work. Once, he brought his trumpet and went into the woods to play. It was thrilling to hear those trumpet tunes floating through the trees. However, they didn't last long. One of the neighbors came up to the house and complained about the noise, so I broke the bad news to Joe that he had to practice in the house.

Playing in the woods was not a new experience for Joe. He had once played in a canoe while visiting his brother Mike and his wife, Diane, on a lake in northern Maine. While he floated along playing his trumpet, a group of loons flew around the canoe listening to his music. When he went back to the cabin, Mike asked him if he had seen the loons. "No," he answered, "I haven't met them yet." He thought Mike was talking about the neighbors.

That fall Joe applied again to Juilliard. At the time, he had a cold sore on his lip, which made playing the trumpet almost impossible. As the judges couldn't see the individuals being auditioned, they had no way of knowing it was Joe. He was turned down. He expected it, but it was another discouraging setback.

He then applied to the Manhattan School of Music. He had already been considering Manhattan because of its emphasis on jazz, which he really wanted to work on more. His lip was better by then. He auditioned for Manhattan and was accepted. One of the judges had also participated at the Juilliard audition. He said to Joe afterward, "Why didn't you audition for Juilliard. We'd love to have you there." Joe didn't tell him that he had, but was turned down. He should have.

Although all his training up to that point had been in classical music, he had started developing an interest in jazz way back in high school. In fact, during those years Joe attended a Wynton Marsalis concert and met him afterward. A few years later when they met again, Wynton recognized Joe and said, "Oh, I remember you from my concert at your town." Joe felt so proud because he looked up to Wynton for his ability to play both classical and jazz.

During Joe's time at Juilliard, he was going steady with a wonderful young lady by the name of DeeAnne. They had known each other since ninth grade and had dated off and on over the years. Their relationship, a beautiful, tender love, was so mature for two young people. I suppose it was unfair that DeeAnne had committed herself to a boy so much in love with his music, but they were inseparable and she seemed not to mind. She frequently drove down to New York to visit Joe, and they wrote and called frequently.

When Joe went to Manhattan, he realized he could not offer DeeAnne much of a future and that she should not keep her life on hold indefinitely. She wanted to marry and have children. Joe was miserable: he was in no position to marry anyone. Yet he loved DeeAnne enough not to hurt her any further. After a long talk one evening, Joe told her that he had no money, no job, no prospect of being able to support a family in the near future, and told her that she should find someone whom she could love and be happy with. They were both crushed by what was unavoidable, but accepted it like mature adults. She took Joe's decision seriously, which he had intended she should, and began dating another young man she deeply admired. Joe was strong enough to follow through on his decision, but it was difficult for him. He prayed, he threw himself even more into his music, which was an outlet for his sadness. Though they had broken up for good, the two remained each other's best friend and constant mutual support.

For many reasons, that was a difficult year. Joe was beginning to find life more and more confusing, and with that came doubts and depression. One day a friend offered him a reefer, which relieved the pain. Gradually, Joe grew to depend on marijuana to lift his spirits, and before long, he was hooked on the stuff. Thus began a new and horrible drama in Joe's life, a nightmare that was to devastate all of us. He finished out the year at Manhattan, but took a sick leave in

November to enter a thirty-day rehabilitation program. I used to visit him with his family. It broke my heart to see him in such a situation. All I could think of was the vulnerable child in him and the innocence that strangers could never understand.

"Why are you crying, Fahd?" Joe would ask me.

I found it difficult to give him an answer. All I could say was, "I don't know, Joe. I guess I just feel your pain and know how brave a step it must be for you to be here."

"You don't think I am the black sheep of the family, do you, Fahd?" he asked so humbly.

"No, Joe, you are not a black sheep. Every one of us falls miserably. Some falls are open for everyone to see. The worst sins are the hidden sins of meanness and cruelty that quietly and secretly destroy others. Your weakness hurts no one, Joe, but yourself, and knowing you since you were a baby, I know how easily you are wounded by the meanness around you, and I cry because I see how deeply that meanness has hurt you. No, you are not a black sheep, Joe. You are a beautiful soul whom God is using in his own strange way to deliver messages to others through your life. I guess sometimes I see too much, Joe, I see the way God is working in you, and it is painful. That's why I cry."

"I love you, Fahd. You're my best friend, after Jesus. You know, Fahd, when I am in New York, there is a church I stop into and just sit there before the altar and cry and pour my heart out to Jesus, asking him to help me. Do you think he hears me?"

"Joe, he's heard you already. Don't you think he was the one who had Rick and Mike pick you up and bring you home and work so hard so you could come here? Don't doubt Jesus' friendship, Joe. He just works silently and in ways we never understand. But he is real, and he is faithful and true. He is always by your side. Don't be afraid!"

"But how can he know about what I am going through, with all the hundreds of millions of people on earth?"

"Joe, look at the sun rising in the morning! Its rays touch all of creation in a single moment. Imagine God's intelligence as the sun's rays. His intelligence scans the whole universe in a single moment and knows every detail about his creation in an instant. It's that simple. When he sees you, Joe, he focuses in on you and is there beside you in a very special way, especially when you approach him in Communion."

Joe spent his Thanksgiving at the rehab center. While there, he befriended a number of others who were hurting as much as himself. He got word to me that he needed *Joshuas*, so I sent them over, autographed. One was for a brilliant young man who told his counselor he did not have a Higher Power. Joe was concerned about him and asked if I would autograph a copy of *Joshua* for him before he went back home to New Jersey. There were at least a dozen others.

Joe finished rehab at the beginning of December. Not long after he came home, he received a phone call from his friend in New Jersey. It was a brief call; the gist of the friend's message was, "Thanks, Joe, I now have a Higher Power. I really loved *Joshua*. It gave me a whole new outlook on life."

Joe returned to the Manhattan School with no questions asked. He did well in his classes, as his record indicates. He had many friends, girls as well as boys, though he didn't have much time for dating. Unfortunately, he did not have enough discipline to attend his AA meetings and gradually slipped back into his addiction. I could tell because he would call every now and then needing money to pay his share of the phone bill or the electric bill or on occasion the rent bill. He was ashamed to call his parents, knowing that he had failed them. I would write the checks to the companies themselves. This way I at least knew the bills were being paid. I was in a rather painful predicament, because as a priest I felt he had a right to a certain confidentiality whenever he called me. He did not want me to share things with his parents. I could not betray his trust by telling them: that would have ended his tie with me and he needed that open line. I was torn, but as I had no concrete evidence that he had slipped back into his old ways, I couldn't share anything definite that his parents did not already know or suspect. I never gave him money for himself except on special occasions like his birthday and a few other important days, so I never felt I was supporting his habit.

When Joe came home that summer, it was a relief. At least he had got through another year, and this time relatively unscathed and with a good academic record at that. He was proud of himself, and everyone was proud of him.

While he was home, I tried to get him to come to Joshua (my place in Altamont) to help with the garden. It was difficult. He had a thousand excuses: he had been out late and needed to sleep in the morning, he had no car, et cetera. His brother John was coming every day to paint the house, however, so he had a ride if he really wanted one. I was worried. I knew he had some kind of a problem, but none of us knew how serious it was.

When he did show up, he was always tired. I would frequently find him stretched out on the grass sound asleep. I would leave him alone. Later on he would come up to the house looking sheepish and apologize.

"Let's get on with it, Joe. You should get more sleep at night. You need your sleep."

He did manage to get a certain amount of work done, but it was minimal. I sensed he was back on drugs. Pushing him to stay awake and work harder would only have increased his guilt and made him stay away from work altogether. At least he was not in trouble while he was at my place. That was worth something. I think Joe felt a sense of peace and did a lot of soul-searching while he was walking around the grounds and lying on the grass. Just his being there in the tranquillity of the mountainside was good therapy for him. And he certainly wasn't concerned about his salary, because half the time he'd forget to collect it.

Earlier that summer Joe went to Round Top, Texas, to attend a music camp. While there he met a bass player by the name of Maria Otero, a delightful young lady from Colombia. During the regular school year she attended Harid Conservatory in Boca Raton, Florida. Joe and Maria became good friends and she talked him into applying to Harid for the fall term. Students accepted there were on full scholarship, and given a modest spending-money allowance over and above their room and board.

When Joe came back home from Round Top, he was again sensing deep feelings of failure and felt himself more than ever a disappointment to his parents. I talked to him, but all he would say was, "Fahd, I may be beaten down again, but the fight is not over. I'm never going to give up. Jesus is still my best friend and I know he is my strength. I'm hurt and ashamed, but I'm not giving up, Fahd, and I know he's going to help me. I just can't understand what he wants. I wish sometimes I could be like everybody else and didn't have to battle so many problems all at once. Fahd, you're like a second father to me and I'm not going to let you down. I'm hangin' in there, no matter how hard it is."

Shortly after, Joe sent his application to Harid and was accepted. Only in writing this manuscript have I been struck by the raw bravery and courage that drove him through all his struggles and obstacles and frustrations with human weakness. The past eleven years of his life had been beset by problems of every sort: the jealousy of teachers less talented than he; his own failure to achieve academically; his shame over the pain he caused his family and me; his struggle to find a relationship that would stabilize his life, with someone with whom he could share his pain and joy; his seeming inability to realize his dreams and ideals; his troubles at music school; his terrifying struggle

with drugs; and his constant fears, which would surface in nightmares that often caused him to wake up
screaming. These things would have destroyed many
young people. But for Joe they were just part of his
normal life and he seemed to accept them.

I felt his pain so often. Many were the nights I
stayed awake worrying about him, and often knowing
beforehand when something terrible was about to
happen, and then begging God to protect him and
help him through whatever trials he had to endure. I
pictured him looking longingly up into the mountains
but unable to move on because he couldn't find the
way. But he never gave up. He reminded me of Will
Stoneman in the movie *Iron Will*, who fought against
unimaginable odds to win the Winnipeg–St. Paul dogsled race. But Joe's struggle was not to win a dogsled
race; his struggle was to conquer himself and resist the
insensitivity of others who in their inability to understand him abandoned him and left him alone to be
destroyed.

So often my memory goes back to those times
when that little boy came running down the street
and leapt up into the air for me to catch him. In his
innocence he treated people with that same abandon,
but there were too many who would not catch him
and turned away when he was falling. Yet he kept
getting up, and finally realized that he would have to

struggle alone. During these times his closeness to Jesus grew deeper. I would catch him by himself just talking to God and listening to God's silent voice, which guided him mysteriously and was the source of his strength. Joe never allowed discouragement or disappointment to overwhelm him. That, I think, was one of the most beautiful and touching facets of his life—his courage in the face of terrifying though unseen enemies.

Alongside his frightful problems there was developing this remarkable spirituality. His tenacious faith, his intimacy with God, the intensity of his pleading, were such an inspiration in a person so young. This was a part of Joe's life not seen by many perhaps, but it was the driving force that carried him through all the stormy nights. Seeing this paradox in Joe gave me a whole new insight: that a person could have frightful, humiliating weaknesses and still be very close to God, deeply in love with God, and able to grow spiritually.

After finishing at Round Top, Maria came to Schenectady to visit Joe and his family. We all became acquainted with her and grew to love this remarkable girl. She and Joe made a striking couple. The fact that the two of them were musicians made a big difference in establishing a compatible relationship, since they had so many things in common. They were at least on the same musical planet. During her stay with Joe's family, they spent time with me at Joshua. Maria helped Joe with his work in the garden. Together we bought a beautiful star magnolia tree about four feet high, which Joe and Maria planted on the lower lawn. They were so proud of that tree. It was a symbol of their newly found relationship.

Eight

O<small>N WEEKENDS THAT SUMMER</small>, Joe played jazz at the Van Dyke, a well-known restaurant in Schenectady. Many people from around the area came to hear him. He often played with his friend Ian, and a few other friends, and sometimes with Norm Frederick and his band. Norm is a lovable man who idolized Joe even though he knew more than anyone about Joe's zany behavior. Sean Lowery and his group also played at the Van Dyke, and Joe would always go to hear them. He had great respect for Sean. Sean liked Joe as well, and whenever he noticed Joe in the audience, he would invite him to play with the group. Sean told me, "He was always fun to be with, and coming home from Juilliard, I could see he had greatly improved in his trumpet playing. He had incredible talent."

During these periods of freedom from school and work, Joe always had time for his friends. There were so many who called him when they were hurting or in trouble, and Joe quietly and surreptitiously helped them, even at the cost of great inconvenience to himself. Sometimes kids would call him in the middle of the night when they needed help, and Joe would always be there for them. His loyalty to his friends was selfless.

When the summer came to an end, Joe went to Florida and entered Harid Conservatory, a really fine school. Maria had an apartment not far from where Joe would be living, so the two would be able to see each other daily.

Joe was in Florida hardly a day when he got himself into serious trouble. He borrowed Maria's car to go to the store, but was arrested while sitting parked on the side of the road ostensibly drinking a can of soda. The police approached the car and arrested him for having something more than Coke in the can. Too ashamed to let his parents know what had happened, Joe wouldn't give the police any information, so they put him in jail. Joe called Maria. Brokenhearted, she immediately called his parents, who then got in touch with me. We were all crushed. What next?

Richard contacted a lawyer in Miami who took over from there and met with Joe. Eventually, Joe was put on probation and allowed to go back to school. But the matter dragged on for days. Joe had to go down to the jail to pay for court expenses by a certain day. When the day came, Maria's car wouldn't start. It was a crisis. A real guardian angel turned up in the person of Joe Gamarano, a friend of mine who took Joe under his wing. He drove over to Joe's place and let him take his car for the trip from Boca Raton to Miami. He also helped Joe and Maria on other occasions, always making himself available.

Joe's fresh start at Harid, so important to him, was already shattered. The dean at the school called Joe into the office and had a long talk with him. He asked Joe to agree to random drug checks during the year. Joe agreed.

Not knowing Joe, and hearing only rumors about him, many of the students shunned him. But even though he got off to a bad start, he excelled in his music, playing solo in concerts and many times first trumpet in the orchestra, as well as in the most difficult chamber music pieces, such as an Alfred Schnittke piece for cello and seven players, performed at the Morikami Museum. At times there were trumpet auditions, in which Joe excelled. When he didn't show up for one of them, Maria called his room to remind him. He had forgotten all about it. With no practice, he went to the audition and arrived just in time for his turn. Not knowing the pieces, he ended up sight-reading; to his and Maria's surprise, he placed first. One of the other trumpet players was very upset, because he had practiced constantly and was determined to beat Joe; however, it was too difficult trying to compete with him. Surprisingly, Joe wasn't the slightest bit interested in beating anyone. Taking the auditions was part of the schedule and he entered as a matter of course.

The same fellow who tried to compete with Joe in the classical audition was certain he could beat him in jazz, since it was in his blood, until one day he happened to hear Joe playing jazz in the practice room. Joe was always pleasant to the fellow, smiling and being lighthearted. Sensitive and warm as he was, Joe found it difficult to have to play so closely with others in the orchestra when they were unfriendly toward him, though one of the boys told Maria that Joe could be the best trumpeter ever if he practiced. Everything came so easily to him. He could sight-read anything perfectly. "I look up to him. I've learned a lot from him," the boy told Maria.

As much as Joe loved his music, he couldn't

wait to come home for Christmas. I don't think anyone could love family and homecoming celebrations
as much as Joe did. The presents he bought were simple things. I usually gave him something to spend on
gifts, but no one expected anything spectacular, as we
all knew he never had much money. Just watching Joe
at Christmastime was a joy in itself. He was like a
child discovering Christmas for the first time.

Usually, Joe played trumpet solos in the midnight Mass at his old church. It was still his birthday
present to the Christ Child. George, the music director there, was a good man, and friendly. Joe liked him
and enjoyed working with him and the choir. I usually
went to the midnight Mass with Richard and Elizabeth and the family. The Mass itself, whether held in
a barn or a cathedral, is always a powerful inspiration
if one looks beyond the externals and plumbs the
depths of the mystery. But it is difficult to describe the
thrill of listening to the sounds that came from Joe's
trumpet. Not only was his playing flawless, but the
feeling, the power, even the tenderness that flowed
from that metal horn were magic to the soul. When
Mass ends, people usually just hurriedly get up and
walk out while the recessional is being played. When
Joe played on those Christmas Eves, people stayed to
listen and were inspired. Everyone knew the music
came from deep inside.

The last time Joe was home for Christmas, George took him home after rehearsal and told him, "Joe, I don't know what I'll do when you're no longer around." To which Joe replied, "Don't worry, George, I'll always be home for Christmas."

Christmas Day was an all-day celebration at the Della Ratta house. No matter what the circumstances, no matter what turmoil, confusion, pains and hurts and anxiety-causing incidents may have happened or were about to happen, Christmas was a day of beauty that no cloud could darken.

Everyone did their part to prepare for the afternoon feast, from Pete and Joey bringing in wood for the wood-burning stove and the fireplaces, and setting the table, to Richard carving the turkey when it was finally ready. Everyone helped—and no one complained.

When Richard's father was alive, his presence was always special. He would bring his accordion and entertain while everyone went about his or her business. Now it was just Richard's mother, Angie. She would never admit to her age, but it was venerable. She occupied center stage, even though it was mostly in the form of good-natured needling while reminiscing over old times.

After Grandpa Della Ratta died, it was Rick and Joe who entertained with their after-dinner music. They patiently played everyone's favorite tunes as long as there was someone to listen. There was a beautiful bond between the two brothers. The music flowed effortlessly from the piano and the trumpet, each player knowing just when to let the other take a solo turn. Rick once remarked to his mother that Joe was the only person who really understood him, and could look into his soul and know what he was thinking and feeling.

All the Della Rattas have a remarkable sense of humor, and their Christmas dinners could well have been televised, with a guarantee to keep the country laughing for hours. Analyzing their happiness, I could easily see that their laughter and joy flowed from a profound realization that who was being celebrated on that day had forever altered their lives.

Joe loved Christmas. He also loved its celebration. So often people celebrate Christmas just to have another reason for a party. Joe loved it because he understood its meaning and because he knew what it meant for him. If he was going to make it, it would only be because of him whose existence he now had to cling to.

When I left the house that evening, I felt a terrible sadness I could not shake, and I began to cry. I was frightened. It was nothing I could put my finger on. It was nothing tangible. I was just frightened, and this fear made me sad. I prayed hard for Joe all the way home.

I usually spend the Christmas holidays by my-self. My house is on a mountain that is covered with snow in an ordinary winter. I like to be alone in the quiet, just sensing God and knowing that Jesus' pres-ence hovers nearby. Not that I feel his presence the way I used to as a young boy, with all the tender emotions and delicate feelings; but rather, with a deep realization that he is near and is an integral part of my life, and has woven mine into his. That Christmas was unusual. I sensed Jesus was telling me something that I could not yet understand. But whatever it was filled me with an inexplicable melancholy. I would wake up in the middle of the night, afraid. I felt Joe's hold on life was very thin.

He returned to Harid after Christmas. When I didn't hear from him, I began to feel a little more secure. Then one night he called and said he owed a lady some money that he had taken. It bothered his conscience terribly and he couldn't rest until he re-paid it.

"I feel so ashamed, Fahd. This lady needed the money more than I did. I never used to have any money and it didn't bother me. But I saw this money lying around and I took it. I am so ashamed. I know she's a poor lady, too, which makes me feel even worse. For some reason I began to think having money was important, I guess because I never had any. Then I started to think about you when you were living in that little house and didn't have any money to live on, and you were happy, and I realized that happiness has to come from inside, not from anything you possess. What you are inside is what makes you happy. When you feel clean inside, that is happiness. When you are good, and feel at peace with God, that is happiness. Whether you have a lot of money or no money at all is irrelevant. It has nothing to do with happiness. If anything, it makes life complicated and destroys our peace of mind."

Joe didn't ask me for the money, but I knew he needed to give it back. I knew he was telling the truth, but I was afraid that if I gave him the money, it might not get to the lady in question, even with the best of intentions. I told Joe I would help him. I then called Maria and asked if she was familiar with what Joe was talking about. She was. So I said I would send her the money, and asked if she would make sure it got to the right person. She said she would. In fact, she and Joe went together to give the money back, and Joe apologized and asked the lady to forgive him. She was very understanding. I felt a sense of relief when Maria called and told me it was taken care of.

The calm did not last long. Unable to sleep,

Maria began calling late at night. As soon as I heard the phone ring, I knew it would be about Joe. "Fahd," Maria would say through her tears, "I am so worried about Joe."

"Maria, what happened?"

It took her the longest time to tell me. Usually, it would be about Joe's staying out late drinking with some of his friends.

"Is he also taking drugs?" I would ask.

"I don't know, I don't think so. He says he's not. I don't know. But he hasn't been himself lately. I don't know what's the matter with him. He is so troubled."

After a number of desperate phone calls, she finally broke down and told me everything that had happened. At the beginning of the second semester, the school gave Joe a random drug test and he failed it. He had passed all the others they'd given him, but not this one. They told him he could not come back the next year. It devastated him. He now had no incentive to take classes. He was adamant about not letting his parents know. Still not giving up, he applied to Florida Atlantic University and was accepted and assigned to first trumpet in the orchestra, which already had a concert scheduled for the fall session. But he was having a very difficult time dealing with another failure.

Maria was an angel to him during these difficult times. She was unable to eat, could not sleep, and even though she was already thin, she was losing weight fast. She managed only with the greatest effort to keep up with her studies and her music. By her sheer love and loyalty to Joe, together with God's grace, she got him through the year.

Joe's playing was still well disciplined, even though he practiced less. He was allowed to play in Harid's concerts, and performed brilliantly, but his spirit was broken and he was trying desperately to put himself back together again.

I talked to him. He sounded really down. I told him I was coming to Boca Raton for a book signing within the next few days and would be staying at the Gamaranos'. I told him I would like to have dinner with him and Maria and the Gamaranos. He was thrilled.

When I arrived, he was in a much better frame of mind, as if he had come to terms with himself and with whatever he had been struggling with. In fact, he was in a lighthearted mood, probably because the school year had ended and he would be going home in a few days. And he was looking forward to Florida Atlantic in the fall.

Before the dinner I had the book signing at a local bookstore. It was a large crowd as usual. Some of my loyal friends came—Dorothy Bunting and a friend of hers, and Lou and Toby Neifeld. It was a happy surprise seeing them there.

After the signing we went to a nice Chinese restaurant. We were all in good spirits, Joe exceptionally so. As soon as the waitress came to our table to take orders, Joe began talking to her in what I took to be fake Chinese. I was embarrassed, and when the waitress was taking my order, I told her not to pay attention to Joe, that he was just clowning around. She looked surprised and said, "No, he speaks beautiful Chinese. He even has the intonation down perfectly, which most Americans find impossible to master."

"Are you serious?"

"Very serious. He speaks wonderful Chinese."

I couldn't believe it.

When the waitress left, I looked at Joe and he had that cherubic grin on his face. "All right, Joe, out with it. What's up with this Chinese bit?"

He finally told us. His roommate was Chinese, and whenever the boy's father called to talk to his son, he was at the library. "I didn't want the father to keep wasting his money by calling like that, so I had my roommate teach me Chinese so I could talk to his father and tell him all about his son. The father was thrilled. That's all, Fahd. I wasn't making fun of the waitress, I really was speaking Chinese."

Then he went on to explain about the different intonations and how the same sound would have an entirely different meaning if you used a different intonation. Before long he had us all in pain from laughing so hard as he illustrated *how* different intonations changed the meaning of the same words. It was Joe at his best. It was so good to see him his normal, happy self again. Maria seemed a lot happier as well. We all had a great time that night.

Nine

J OE CAME HOME AT THE END OF MAY, and in the middle of June he started working at Joshua. There was a noticeable difference in his personality. He came to work early, and worked with enthusiasm. I wanted to get an early start on my vegetable garden, so Dave Bogatka, the gardener, rototilled the ground to make it easy for us to mix in the compost. The garden was now three times larger than when Joe had first worked on it three years earlier.

"Fahd, this garden is *big*. Remember when we first dug it up? It seemed impossible. This is great,

Fahd. It'll be a piece of cake this year. What shall we plant?"

"What would you like to plant?"

"How about the white corn again, and tomatoes, and peppers, and lettuce, and cucumbers, and melons. We never had any luck with melons. Why don't we try them again? Did you save the seeds from those delicious melons you bought, the ones from Israel and Mexico?"

"Yes, I have them inside. I also have some from the melons we bought from the Hand melon farm. We'll plant some of each and see what happens. I'd like to try planting them against the back of the house this year. It is warmer there at night and I think they need hot nights to grow well."

"Fahd, look! The strawberry plants we planted two years ago are doing great. They've got blossoms all over them. Does that mean we're going to get a lot of strawberries?"

"It sure does, Joe. The only problem will be beating the crows and the chipmunks in the morning. I'll put a mesh over them."

With the two of us working together, everything was planted in a few days. We were both proud of the garden. Joe came each day and faithfully watered it, developing his own little system of caring for the garden. It showed he was interested.

When we finished the vegetable garden, we zeroed in on the flower garden and the rose garden. Dave did the bulk of the work during the year, sometimes with his friend John Drudis, and kept the grounds in beautiful shape; but when Joe came home, Dave tended to the important things and turned over the flower gardens to Joe and myself. Joe loved working with the flowers. His favorites were the portulacas. He went wild over them—they were so quaint and colorful, and so abundant. He planted them all over the place. We had practically every kind of popular flower you could think of that summer. The perennial garden was lush with new growth and fully matured plants. Though the rose garden had suffered greatly from winterkill, and new plants were needed to fill the empty spaces, it was still beautiful. The other garden beds spread out around the grounds were much more extensive than before, and Joe was thrilled to be able to work on them. His brother Peter came home from school and also helped, though I needed him more to make tapes of talks I had been giving. At times he worked in the garden, but didn't particularly like it. Three years earlier he had told me, "Fahd, I'm really not into hard work." But since then he's come a long way, and feels much more comfortable in the garden, especially after he began to see his hard work flourish with such striking colors.

Joe and Dave worked together much of the time. We had my good friend John Pollard bring truckloads of compost, which kept Joe, Dave and Pete busy for weeks in the blazing heat.

One day Joe asked if his friend Tony Speranza could chip in. I thought it was a good idea. He and Joe had been friends for years, ever since their days together in the Empire State Youth Orchestra, in which Tony also played trumpet. Besides being an excellent trumpet player, Tony was a big help in the garden. The little team worked well together. My brother, Ed, who had retired from a career in psychiatry, was a genius at landscaping, which I was really hoping he would concentrate on here. However, he was busy putting a new cedar roof over my wraparound porch.

I had work to do inside, so I just supervised occasionally and kept an eye on things as I walked around. Joe really applied himself and was excited about the way things were going, even during the intense heat. I knew he had finally beaten the drug habit. Even though we had beer in the house, Joe drank only soda or iced tea. It was such a joy seeing him at peace and happy, and free again.

But one day, in early summer, he came into the house looking dejected.

"Joe, what's the matter?"

"Fahd, you know the tree Maria and I planted last year, is it still alive? It looks dead."

"I don't know, Joe. Let's go down and have a look."

We walked down the driveway to the lower lawn and to the spot where they had planted the tree, which had been four feet high and beautifully shaped. Now there was nothing there but debris. I felt bad.

I got down on my hands and knees and secretly said a prayer as I carefully scratched around in the mulch. I raked my fingers gently through the debris and uncovered a tiny shoot about an inch and a half high.

"Joe, it's not dead," I said excitedly as I looked up at him. "Look, here's a little shoot coming up."

"Fahd, I'm so glad. That tree is a symbol of Maria and myself. It almost died, didn't it? I guess our relationship almost died, too. Fahd, you have the knack of reviving things that are dying. Do you think you can revive this little tree?"

"Let's see what we can do, Joe. First of all, this little shoot has developed a strong, healthy root system. It has to grow. The soil here is rock and clay. That's bad. You might want to dig a trench around it and fill it with that black dirt from the pile. That will make it easy for the roots to expand. Then, make sure you water it every day."

"Will it come back?"

"It'll come back, Joe. Don't worry! It's a healthy little shoot."

Each day Joe faithfully watered that shoot. Each day it grew bigger and stronger.

The weeks passed by lazily. It was a hot summer, the hottest in many years. Joe worked in the gardens, bare-chested and perspiring. He developed a nice tan.

"This is good work, Fahd. It's fun working in the dirt. You know, when I get out of school and settled in a symphony orchestra, and have a family, I'm going to have a garden on my land. I want to have a house with a nice piece of land, so I can spend time working in my garden and growing vegetables and flowers. I never realized what fun working in the garden could be. You taught me a lot, Fahd. You really are my best friend."

"Thanks, Joe. We've been friends for a long time."

We started two new gardens that summer. The first one was down on the second lawn in front of the house, on the other side of the driveway. It will eventually be an enclosed garden where people can spend quiet time while on retreat. A four-hundred-foot walkway winds its way through the lawn at present. Joe and Dave and Pete, and later on, Tony Speranza, worked on it all summer, carving it out of the grass. When they finished, they planted little flowerbeds all along the walk, from the driveway (where it begins) to the gazebo (where it ends). That was hard work, as the soil there is clay and rock.

The second garden was around the small pond on the hill up in back of the house. One of my nephews, Steve Petrie, constructed Japanese bridges for the two ends of the pond, one going over the spillway from the well, the other at the opposite end, where the overflow empties into a creek. The last thing Joe did that summer was plant flowers around those bridges.

All summer long flowers bloomed everywhere. First came the crocuses, then the daffodils and hyacinths. Next came the tulips and lilacs and irises and peonies. Finally, the perennials appeared with their vast array of color. Joe loved them all, but as I've mentioned, the portulacas were his favorite. He would sing songs to them as soon as he got out of the car in the morning. We all just stood around and laughed. Whatever Joe did to those plants, they flourished; in fact, everything he touched flourished. I couldn't believe it. It was as if God had just overwhelmed him with love and reassurance. We planted corn together in two plots right next to each other. By the middle of July his was six feet tall; mine, or whatever of it survived the rodent attacks, was only three feet tall. Joe would laugh, "Fahd, you just don't have the touch. I'll have to show you how to do it. You have to sing to them and tell them you love them and they thrive, you know, Fahd, just like human beings?"

He could be zany sometimes, but it was so good to see him happy and full of fun again. One day I walked out on the porch. Joe was sitting there looking out across the valley, deep in thought.

"Joe, you look like you're a thousand miles away. What are you thinking about?"

"Oh, just thinking about God. God is so good, Fahd. All these beautiful flowers that grow around here. They show how tender God is. He could have created everything in black and white. He didn't have to create all these beautiful things. And that valley spread out before us as far as you can see. It is so breathtaking. I can feel God all around me. I get more of a high from all these beautiful things God has given us for free than from the most powerful drugs."

That was all he said. It was precious. He had turned the corner. Each day Joe would make little remarks like that which evidenced an intimacy with God exploding within him. The things he felt most strongly about he rarely talked about. As his closeness to God deepened, he spoke less about it, but the little remarks showed something beautiful happening inside.

At about that time I was working on *Joshua and the City*. I was typing the chapter about Satan. It was one-thirty in the morning and the phone rang. It was a stranger from a faraway country who started telling me about the devil and how he was working among some of her friends, and the terrible things that were happening. I felt sorry for the poor woman and tried to help as best I could over the telephone, but when I hung up, I had such a feeling of fright. I could sense a subtle, subliminal message, totally unintended by the person who called. The message: "Don't interfere in what the devil is trying to accomplish or you will pay the price."

I was frightened, but I knew I had to continue writing, so I did. I finished that chapter and the following chapters and was able to keep working my way to the end of the manuscript.

The days that followed were ordinary. The annual retreat held nearby at Pyramid Lake was well attended. Sister Dorothy Ederer and I directed it together. She had gotten lots of experience working with people on retreat in her work as a campus minister out at Western Michigan University. She was a real natural at it. I realized more than ever how much she was needed for my ministry of bringing Jesus to others. I asked her if she would consider working further with me and she said she would think it over.

After the retreat she and the musicians who came with her from Kalamazoo stayed at my house for the next day or so. There they met Joe. Dorothy enjoyed his playful humor, and commented afterward, "Joe is such a free spirit. When he played at the Van Dyke that night, I was in awe of his playing. When I watched him, all I could think of was a free-spirited, dancing musical note. He was a breath of fresh air."

Toward the end of July, Maria came to visit Joe and his family in Schenectady. They came to Joshua and spent the day together. Maria worked in the gardens with Joe. They were like two little kids in love. Maria was much more relaxed and at peace and I could tell their relationship was back on track. She returned to the music camp at Chautauqua after the weekend for her last week there. On Monday, Joe came to work as usual. The next day he asked if he could have the next three days off to visit Maria. I was surprised.

"Joe, she was just here this past weekend, and she is coming back this weekend for good. Why do you have to go all the way out there when she's coming back so soon?"

"I don't know, Fahd. All I know is that I have to see her."

"Okay, Joe, if you feel it is that important. Do you have enough money? Here, take this, and be careful driving."

Tony Speranza was working with Joe that day, and as they were finishing up, Joe gave him a big hug and kissed him on the mouth. Tony was shocked and said so. Joe came into the house a few minutes later and told me what he had done and asked if it was all right. He told me how taken aback Tony was. "I told him he was my best friend, after you, Fahd, but he was still shocked."

I laughed and said there was nothing wrong with it, though men didn't usually show affection for each other in that way. "Don't worry about it, Joe. There was nothing wrong with it. You are just very affectionate and demonstrative."

Tony was probably Joe's closest friend. He had been teaching that summer at the New York State Music Camp in Oneonta. In between sessions he would visit Joe at his home in Schenectady. The two of them would practice duets for hours on end. Tony liked practicing with Joe because he said he could learn so much from him. It was especially good for Joe, since it helped keep him focused on his music.

The two of them often participated in jam sessions at the Van Dyke and other jazz clubs in the area.

Joe went to visit Maria at Chautauqua. I finished my manuscript that Thursday and sent it out overnight to my publisher. He received it the next day.

On Saturday I had to drop off some papers for Joe's father, who is my lawyer. On the way down my driveway I noticed that Joe's star magnolia tree looked different. I drove over to it, and to my surprise it had a beautiful white flower on the top. It had bloomed three months out of season. I drove over to the Della Rattas. Joe was home. He had returned the night before from visiting Maria, and also Tony on his way back. He had had a wonderful few days. He thanked me for giving him the time off. He gave me a big hug and told me he had just played at a wedding in Amsterdam, and had to leave in a little while to go up past Lake George to play at another wedding with Norm Frederick and his group. I wished him well and left.

The rest of the day was ordinary. I went back to the house and worked and went to bed at about eleven-thirty. At one-thirty the phone rang. It was Norm Frederick. He was beside himself.

"What's the matter, Norm? Calm down. What happened?"

"I can't tell you."

"What do you mean, you can't tell me. What happened? Is it Joey?"

"Yes."

"What happened to him?"

"The worst. It was a car accident."

"Is he dead?"

"I think so."

I thought an arrow had been shot through my heart. I had never felt such pain, such grief, such total devastation.

Norm continued, "The reason I called you is because I can't get myself to tell his parents. Can you tell them? The state police are going to call and tell them, but I thought it would be better coming from you, since you are so close to them."

I had a hard time agreeing to do it, but I told him I would. I spoke to Norm for a few minutes trying to calm him. He had been close to the family since he was a young boy. The two families had been friends for years. They came from Italy together.

I said a brief prayer for Joe and then called his parents. Elizabeth answered the phone.

When I heard Liz's voice, all I could say was, "Liz, Joey's had an accident."

Thinking it was just a fender bender, she asked, "He did? Where is he?"

"He's in heaven. Joey's gone home."

She merely said, "Oh no!"

There was nothing more to say. That brief exchange said it all. I hung up, broke down and cried my heart out, and prayed for Joe's peaceful passage home. All of a sudden the past couple of months made such sense. God had brought Joe through his drug crisis, then to the peak of his life; and when he had turned himself in the right direction, God took him home, where he no longer would be prey to the pain and meanness around him, and where he could be happy and at peace forever, playing whatever equivalent to a trumpet was popular in that place of joyful music.

I wanted to be with Richard and Elizabeth and went with them to the hospital in Saratoga. It was the most difficult time of our lives. Norm Frederick was there and told us that after the wedding he and the rest of the band had gone to a restaurant to get something to eat. Joe opted out since he wanted to go right home so that he could get up early and go to the Yankee game in New York the next day. It was at least a sixty-mile drive back to Schenectady. There was a heavy fog on the Northway, but at that time of the night, practically no cars. The state troopers estimated that the car was not going fast, but Joe must have seen a deer crossing the highway because the car swerved sharply to the right as if trying to avoid hitting something, then went off the road and hit a tree. Joe was killed immediately.

We stayed at the hospital long enough for the family to identify the body. Then we left. It was the most horrible ride of my whole life. We arrived back at the house and Elizabeth awakened Peter; he was the only one at home. When she told him what had happened, the poor boy was beside himself with grief. The two brothers had become very close in the past year and Pete had just reached the age where they could enjoy doing things together. Pete cried his heart out. It was heart-wrenching to see. I felt so helpless.

I stayed a few minutes longer, then drove back home to Joshua. I could hardly see the way through the tears. By the time I reached the house, it was dawn. I went inside for a few minutes, then went out into the garden and wept. All I could think of was that frightening phone call about the devil at one-thirty in the morning, and the phone call about Joe at one-thirty in the morning. "Oh my God, no!"

I knew in my heart that God would never give Satan the power over someone's life. But the thought and the coincidence were paralyzing.

"Joey, Joey, Joey! You have to give me a sign. You have to give me a sign. You have to let me know you're okay and at peace," I pleaded in my anguish.

"God, I never ask you for anything, because I

trust your love for us so much, but you have to give me a sign. You have to let me know Joey is with you. Dear Lord, you have to give me a sign."

An hour later I got a telephone call from Australia, from a rough, unpolished priest friend, who had problems in his own life but who was a good priest and had started a family program that over the years has helped hundreds of thousands of people in many countries.

"Hi, mate," the voice said.

"Who is this?"

"It's your friend, the Aussie from the outback, Peter McGrath."

"What do you want, Peter?" I said, trying to match his lightheartedness.

"You're hurtin', mate, aren't you?"

"How do you know, Peter?"

"The same voice that told you to call me when I was dying two months ago told me to call you. You're hurtin', aren't you, mate?"

"Peter, I have never hurt so much in my life."

"Tell me about it, mate!"

I told him about Joey. I told him about the tree blooming so late out of season, but I didn't tell him about asking God for a sign.

"You damn fool, mate. God's trying to give you a sign and you're too damn thick to see it. There's a sign from God right under your bloody eyes and you don't even notice it. Open your eyes, mate. God's trying to tell you something. Well, I got to get back to work, mate. I'll see you in October." And he hung up.

I knew Joey was with God.

Ten

THE NEXT FEW DAYS WERE MOST PAINFUL. Dave, the gardener, was devastated. For Dave, who knew Joe so well from bearing with him through each summer, then seeing the transformation the last summer, it was difficult to believe he was dead. The joyful, apparently carefree spirit that brightened everyone else's spirits was no more. Joe's friends were also in a state of disbelief. They could not fathom the demise of someone so full of life and on the threshold of a brilliant career.

But it was only too true. Joe's brothers had a most difficult time. Rick was inconsolable. He had been looking forward to Joe's doing a joint concert with him in New York City, at which Joe was scheduled to play Rick's new composition, "Joshua's Song," already popular, particularly among college students.

Michael, too, was beside himself. John may have seemed the most stoic, but to this day he can't bring himself to talk about Joe. In fact, none of the boys can. Even though they had their rough times together, they also played and hiked and skiied and vacationed together. They were inseparable. To think of Joe as gone was beyond belief. To talk about it as a fact is still too painful.

Elizabeth wanted to know everything there was to know about the accident. Had Joe been driving too fast? Had he been drinking? Had he taken drugs? Had he fallen asleep? The answers to all of the above proved to be negative. There was dense fog on the highway in that particular spot. It was also a deer-crossing area. There were no guard rails or fences on the side of the highway to prevent the animals from crossing. The state police who arrived at the accident scene surmised that Joe most probably saw a deer dart out of nowhere in front of the car, then swerved immediately to avoid hitting it and ran into a tree.

Andy Gigliotti, a funeral director and a good friend of both the family and myself, took care of all the arrangements. It was decided to cremate the remains. Andy and his wife, Theresa, and their loyal associate, my good friend Vittorio Amadei, were a great comfort during those days.

The wake began early because a large crowd was expected. The number of people waiting to console the family was far beyond what anyone could have imagined. People came from all over. The line stretched for over three blocks—young people, old people and many in between. There were people of every color and description. There were blind people and deaf people. Many people no one even knew. There were students of many different backgrounds—Chinese, Japanese, African-American and Spanish—who told Joe's parents how kind he had been to them when they needed someone to care. Joe always seemed to notice when a person was hurting, and would reach out to help in whatever way he could. The guiding inspiration from his childhood he faithfully carried through his whole life: "I should try to see Jesus in each person I meet, and ask how Jesus would want me to treat that person." Whatever difficulties Joe got into, or however complicated his life might have been, he always treated every person he met the way he thought Jesus would have wanted him to.

The wake, therefore, was a stunning testimony to the quiet, unassuming goodness that inspired Joe's relationships with everyone who became involved in his life. One person after another came up to Richard and Elizabeth and told them how much Joe had meant to them when they were troubled and sometimes desperate. One blind musician remembered how his teachers never paid much attention to him, and how Joe noticed it and used to go to the boy's house and teach him to play the trumpet. Now he was a professional trumpet player, thanks to Joe. Other musicians came from far and wide to pay their respects, each one expressing their admiration for Joe's extraordinary talent. Then there was the young girl who had once sent Joe a birthday card in braille, and later taught him how to read the raised dots so that she could correspond with him. Their friendship lasted from high school right to the end.

People from Joe's school came to offer their condolences. Those teachers who had really known and loved him were brokenhearted. Neighbors came and told Richard and Elizabeth how they always knew when Joe was home from college; they could hear his trumpet playing through their backyards and used to turn their TVs off and open their windows and listen to the strains of Joe's beautiful music. "It is going to be very painful not hearing those joyful trumpet tunes floating through the air on the cool summer nights," they said.

The day of the funeral was the most difficult moment in my life. Father John Provost and I offered the Mass together. I preached the sermon, trying to express from my heart what I knew of Joey since his infancy. I traced the growth of his spirituality through all its stages as he was drawn deeper and deeper into Jesus' life by his own peculiar crucifixion, and I explained how his frightful human weaknesses in no way diminished the beauty of his childlike friendship with Jesus. In fact, his closeness to Jesus grew stronger and stronger as those weaknesses made him ever more aware of how much he needed Jesus' strength and guidance. So often preachers teach that if you really love God, you won't sin. That is so unreal. Look at St. Peter. I don't think anyone could ever love Jesus the way St. Peter loved him, and yet after being with Jesus for three years, often day and night, when the chips were down and Peter became frightened, he denied he ever knew Jesus—and this was barely an hour after he had made his first Communion at the Last Supper. Was Peter still Jesus' friend? Of course he was. Jesus' friendship isn't that shallow. All our friends have flaws, even serious ones, but we still love them. It was the same with Joe and Jesus. It was in his deepest failings that he was closest to God, and although it may have taken him years to find the strength to overcome them, he knew his friendship with Jesus was stronger than ever because of his troubles. He thought more frequently of him and clung to him with greater persistence, precisely because he needed him so much.

After the funeral, Joe's remains were buried on the lower lawn of my front yard next to the star magnolia tree that he and Maria had planted. That beautiful little tree bloomed again the day Joe was buried.

The grave is well taken care of. Dave watches over it like a brother. Joe's dying left a deep void in his heart. Richard and Liz come by frequently with Justy. The first time, Justy just lay there quietly next to the grave, and for the longest time, as if he somehow sensed his friend's presence. Maria comes up from Florida each vacation and spends hours at the grave just thinking and reading over letters from long ago. DeeAnne and her mother stop by often and leave flowers there.

One day a musician in his late forties came to visit Joe's grave. I asked him what older musicians drew from Joe's life. His response was, "Father, I learned more music from Joe than I did in music school. But what I really learned from Joe was how to live. That boy had a depth of spirituality unlike anything I have ever seen. I can't tell you how I will miss him. And so will many others."

After the funeral I had a chance to talk to

Maria. I asked her about Joe's visit with her at Chautauqua and what he was like then.

"I had never seen Joe so peaceful as he was those three days," she remembered. "He kept talking about God, and how good God was. He must have had an experience of God in some way. Whenever he would see a flower, he would go over to it and look at it and remark, 'How beautiful this flower is, my little princess! It is so delicate and so full of joy. God gave us these flowers as his way of saying, "I love you."' "

"We took the boat rides around the lake. Joe was so gentle and so tender. We talked about music and about how thrilled he was at going to Florida Atlantic and playing first trumpet in the orchestra.

"We went to Chinese restaurants, which he loved. We had so much fun those few days. It was Joe back to his real, beautiful self. I felt so good about our love. I fell in love with him all over again. I knew he had conquered his habit. I think his visit was his way of reassuring me of that."

Epilogue

J OE'S GOING HOME has left a terrible void in our
hearts, a void well expressed by Ken McElligott, a
good friend of mine and of Joe's family. He knew Joe
from the day he was born and used to babysit for him.
The poem he sent to Richard and Elizabeth, entitled
"Missing Joey," expresses poignantly the feelings of so
many:

> *Death came like a thief in the night.*
> *He took away a priceless soul,*
> *And left behind*

Incredible pain,
Incredible grief,
Incredible silence,
Incredible emptiness.

Everyone says,
"Why? Why? Why? Why?
Why to such a beautiful person?
Why to such a beautiful family?
Why stop such beautiful music?
Why in such a frightening manner?"

Death turns and speaks:
"I do my job.
I must take all of you.
Some early, some late.
You have your cherished memories
To comfort you
Until you see Joey again,
As your Master told you.
Or don't you believe Him?"

Everyone answers,
"We believe, we believe,
But it still hurts so much."

Joe's joyful spirit still floats around in our memories. But beyond this, his life has taught us all so many things we needed to know. I think every life preaches a message. God's purpose in placing us here is so that we can enrich each other's lives. No matter what genius or talent we may have, in God's eyes that is not the work of our life. It may be a facet of who we are, but it is not the essential reason for our existing, which is to find God and to learn to know God—and in getting to know him, to fall in love with him. As we fall in love with him, our personality gradually transforms.

So often it is our sins and our shameful weaknesses that make God real to us in a way we have never experienced before. We may have known him and even loved him, but so often our weaknesses impel us to cling to God, and in clinging to him we feel the strength and power of his infinitely tender love. For the first time, we know what is God's tender mercy. The bond that develops is tougher than steel, binding us to him so powerfully that nothing can separate us ever again.

With all Joe's struggling to conquer his addiction, he still failed. Most humans gave up on him. Only Maria stayed by his side in his moments of desperation, until God finally decided to give him the grace. When that happened, from then on all was easy and his life became light as a feather and filled with joy again. If we have virtue and goodness, it is because God gives us the grace. Our struggles without it are in vain.

Once Joe received that gift, and his life changed almost overnight, it was as if Jesus said to him, "Joe, you have fought the good fight. You have been scarred and bruised and shamed and humbled, but through it all you have remained loyal to me and clung to our friendship. The real work of your life is now over. Your music was my gift to you so that you could give joy to others along the way, but in my plan that was not to be your real calling. Developing your friendship with me was the real purpose of your life, and showing others how faithful my friendship can be when they are troubled—that was what I wanted you to manifest to the world. You did that well. Now I want you to come home with me, Joe. It is beautiful here. You can see me face to face, and meet my Father, and be filled with my Spirit, and meet my mother, and all my friends, and be filled with a joy and happiness you could never imagine. Your loved ones will never be very far away, just on the other side of the veil. You will watch them and see the beautiful way I work in their lives, and understand. There is also music here, music such as you have never heard on earth, and you will be part of it, playing to your heart's content. So come home, Joe, and be at peace. Though you may have tripped and fallen along the way, you never gave up, and you have won the race."

And so God took Joe home.

Good-bye, Joe, my little friend!